CLASSIC
SOURDOUGHS

CLASSIC
A Home Baker's Handbook
SOURDOUGHS

Ed Wood

Ten Speed Press
Berkeley • Toronto

A Kirsty Melville Book

Ten Speed Press
PO Box 7123
Berkeley, California 94707
www.tenspeed.com

Distributed in Australia by Simon and Schuster Australia, in Canada
by Ten Speed Press Canada, in New Zealand by Southern Publishers Group,
in South Africa by Real Books, in Southeast Asia by Berkeley Books,
and in the United Kingdom and Europe by Airlift Book Company.

Cover design by Jeff Puda
Interior design by Tasha Hall
Front cover photo by Aaron Wehner
Special thanks to Sur La Table for kindly
loaning props for front cover photo.

Library of Congress Cataloging-in-Publication Data
on file with the publisher.
ISBN 1-58008-344-7

First printing 2001
Printed in the United States of America

3 4 5 6 7 8 9 10 — 05 04 03

CONTENTS

Acknowledgments   *vii*

Preface   *ix*

Introduction   *xi*

Chapter 1 ≈ *The Birth and Life of Sourdough*   1

Chapter 2 ≈ *The Ingredients of Sourdough Bread*   8

Chapter 3 ≈ *Putting It All Together*   34

Chapter 4 ≈ *Recipes*   50

Chapter 5 ≈ *Baking Sourdoughs in Bread Machines*   167

Chapter 6 ≈ *Wild Cultures from Sourdoughs International*   184

Appendix   *199*

Selected Sources   *203*

Bibliography   *204*

Index   *205*

About the Author   *210*

ACKNOWLEDGMENTS

Many people, from the deserts of Saudi Arabia to the mountains of Idaho, have participated in baking and taste tests of the recipes in this book. Their comments and suggestions will surely enhance the final product in your kitchen.

In the last five years, my life has been enriched enormously by contacts with individuals engaged in the production of ingredients that have transformed the sourdoughs described in this book. In subsequent chapters, I will introduce you to Glenn and Linda Pizzey, who acquainted me with flax at their Manitoba mill. Michael Orlando of Sunnyland Mills educated me on the virtues and current status of bulgur. Joe Vanderliet traveled all the way from San Leandro, California, to investigate this strange sourdough enterprise on an Idaho mountain, and he brought me up to speed on the organic flours produced at his Certified Foods.

Perhaps most warming has been the steady input from readers of the 1996 edition *World Sourdoughs from Antiquity;* their comments on how much their lives have been transformed by their introduction to my world of sourdoughs have put me in their debt. Your comments, as a new reader, will be welcome as well.

My wife, Jean, did the original proofing and editing and the complete electronic production of the manuscript.

PREFACE

I frequently ask myself why people around the world are again becoming interested in sourdoughs. I see evidence of it almost daily here at Sourdoughs International where we grow, harvest, and dry cultures that Jean and I collect from around the world. Orders for those cultures come from places as far afield as South Africa, Japan, Australia, and Norway. The simple answer is that, in many ways, sourdoughs improve the quality of our lives. They have a unique, inherent charisma, and they still produce the best bread the world has ever known. They are soul satisfying and fun: I call them "endorphins of the kitchen." They truly offer a moment of personal quality extending beyond what we eat to what we do and to what we are.

Eleven years ago, I self-published *World Sourdoughs from Antiquity*. In 1996, it was revised, and Ten Speed Press did a much better job with it than I did. This book borrows from both versions, but updates the materials with what I have learned in eleven years from readers and critics. I have learned a lot, and in these pages you will find many changes, including new ways to do old sourdoughs. The purpose of this book is the same as ever: to share with you the pleasure and enrichment of using sourdoughs in your own kitchen.

INTRODUCTION

Let's start by defining what I really mean by "traditional" sourdoughs. We know the sourdough process results from the fermentation reactions of two quite different classes of microorganisms, wild yeast and beneficial bacteria. For well over five thousand years, all breads were produced by the fermentation of these two essential microorganisms acting together. The yeasts are primarily responsible for leavening and bread texture; the bacteria for the sourdough flavor. Thus the definition of "traditional" sourdough requires a "culture," or "starter," containing both these organisms. I place particular emphasis on the term *wild* since the commercial bread industry has developed new yeast strains that are incompatible with sourdoughs. Why incompatible? The new yeasts ferment so rapidly that the dough is leavened and baked before the bacteria have time to produce the sourdough flavor. Commercial bakers love saving time since it is possible to produce more bread at less cost and more profit. But the loss of sourdough flavor and texture means the total loss of sourdoughs, as I define them, and the result is inferior bread.

Delicious, nutritious breads of various kinds were produced for centuries by a process no one understood. Bakers believed there was "something" in dough that made it rise. They knew if they saved some old dough and added it to a new batch, the new dough would also rise. For eons, all new doughs required a bit of old dough to "start" the rising process. In villages around the world, bread literally supported life. It was the staff of life. They baked it in their homes and every town had a baker and a bakery where the people could take their dough to be baked or buy it. When the pioneers emigrated to this country, they brought their dough starters with them. The California forty-niners and the Yukon and Alaskan miners get credit for the term *sourdoughs*, probably due to the extreme flavor of their breads. They subsequently became known as sourdoughs themselves. Thus my definition of "traditional" sourdough also requires a culture with organisms that, with proper care, will survive and replicate themselves forever.

In the early 1800s, Pasteur looked into a microscope and saw what we now call wild yeast and discovered for the first time what really made bread dough rise. About a hundred years later researchers learned how to select, isolate, and grow single strains of yeast in pure cultures. They searched for and found species of *Saccharomyces cerevisiae,* baker's yeast, that leavened bread doughs with incredible speed.

Then the industrial revolution took bread out of the home and put it in factories that manufacture something labeled "bread" that neither looks like nor tastes like the staff of life. Breads began to be produced by mammoth machines. Sourdough starters were no longer used, small town bakeries disappeared, people stopped baking in their home, and the staff of life became neither delicious nor nutritious. Bakers thought the need for sourdough cultures was gone forever, but they were wrong. Baker's yeast is totally incapable of producing the sourdough flavor and without the lactobacilli the quality of breads has never been the same.

Within just the last hundred years there have been monumental changes to what we call bread, and these changes are mostly bad.

Huge baking machines now dominate the production of bread. In addition, the baking industry adds a plethora of chemicals to change the physical characteristics of flour and dough to improve their "machinability." These include surface-active agents (surfactants) to help doughs go through machinery without sticking or tearing, other chemicals to soften the final bread texture or strengthen the dough by modifying the gluten, and a host of emulsifiers just to improve the mixing characteristics or increase shelf life. All of these special additives have one thing in common: No, or very limited, nutritional value. At least one of them, potassium bromate, has been banned worldwide as a potential carcinogen. Large baking conglomerates are typified by the Interstate Bakeries Corporation, the largest wholesale baker and distributor of fresh delivered bread in the United States. In 1997, their annual sales were $3.12 billion with a net profit of $100 million from sixty-seven bakeries and thirty-two thousand employees. Their distribution network delivers to over two hundred thousand retail outlets on ten thousand delivery routes. A substantial amount of their bread is delivered as either refrigerated or frozen dough, which local bakeries warm up or thaw and bake. There is nothing necessarily bad about that except the frozen doughs contain all the additives and chemicals included by the wholesale producers to grease their progress through the massive machinery.

The deterioration of bread quality is a worldwide phenomenon. In an elegant description in *Smithsonian* magazine (January 1995), Rudolph Chelminski tells the story of the dismal decline of French bread, which he credits in part to "good old greed." The story is not greatly different on this side of the ocean.

In spite of these monumental changes, a small cadre of hardy souls continued using the old-fashioned sourdough methods and today are on the comeback trail as "artisan" bakeries. They persist in baking traditional sourdoughs, and they find a ready market for their products. One example is the French Meadow Bakery in Minneapolis, owned and operated by Lynn Gordon. Gordon started baking organic sourdoughs in 1985. She now produces twenty thousand loaves of organic naturally leavened bread each week and approximately two million loaves a year in twenty-two different varieties. And she appears to be doing so with financial success.

The best breads available today are being produced in the home or in artisan bakeries. But in our kitchens, the techniques are not the same as those used by the artisan bakers, or by the pioneers. The early bakers used their starters to bake almost every day. Most of us start with a culture that has become dormant between uses. The production capacity of the artisan baker requires masonry or special ovens and equipment beyond the scope of the individual home baker. For that reason, this book is designed specifically for and dedicated to the individual who bakes for him or herself or for a family and who deserves the thrill and joy of traditional sourdoughs.

THE BIRTH AND LIFE
Chapter 1
OF SOURDOUGH

It took uncounted centuries for wheat and other grains used for flour to evolve. Jarmo, in the uplands of Iraq, is one of the oldest archaeological excavations in the Middle East, dating to about 8,000 B.C. Here, archaeologists have identified carbonized kernels and clay imprints of plants that resemble wild and domesticated wheats. Historians believe that similar grains were established in Egypt by at least the same time, and perhaps as early as 10,000 to 15,000 B.C. Rye existed in the Middle East as an unwanted weed and eventually spread across the Mediterranean to the Baltic countries, where it dominates bread making to this day. These wild grasses took millennia to progress to grain-producing plants, and it was centuries before humans learned to cultivate and use them for food.

Grains like wheat and rye were probably first consumed as porridge. Eventually, this gruel evolved into a flat cake of baked cereal—baked perhaps on a hot rock in the fire. But how did these flat, hard cakes rise for the first time and become bread? An unbaked cake, perhaps forgotten on a warm summer evening, would be a perfect medium for contamination by an errant wild yeast. Imagine how many times that accident occurred before someone saw it and then baked it! It must have taken a thousand years, a thousand accidents, and finally a thousand experiments to produce a recognizable loaf of bread.

The Discovery of Yeast

In 1676, a Dutch lens grinder, Anton van Leewenhoek, first observed and described microscopic life, and in 1680 produced the first sketches of yeast in beer. But nothing more happened for the next 170 years. The first alternative to wild sourdough yeast was obtained from beer foam. Then came Louis Pasteur in 1857, with his proof that fermentation is caused by yeast. A comprehensive system of yeast classification, which we still use, was published in 1896.

With Pasteur's discovery, a whole new field of yeast technology and cereal chemistry came to life. Microbiologists learned how to isolate single yeast cells and to select pure cultures. They selectively bred wild strains to develop yeast cells that leavened faster, were more tolerant to temperature change, and were easier to produce commercially. Mass-produced cakes of pressed yeast and packages of active dried yeast contained billions of cells that were all exactly alike. These purified strains are now carefully guarded to prevent contamination by wild types.

Cereal chemists learned to control the texture and appearance of bread by bleaching and blending different types of flour. They found a host of chemical additives to improve the consistency of dough and change its flavor, and to increase the shelf life of the finished loaf and improve its nutritional value. Agronomists selected and bred wheats that resist disease, produce bigger yields per acre, contain more protein, and so on. These advances contributed to the industrial production of bread, with huge machines producing thousands of loaves per day. Now a handful of very large bakeries produce more than three-fourths of all bread sold in the United States. These same "advances" have also led to much of modern bread having the flavor of an edible napkin.

Yeasts are microfungi and are much larger than most bacteria. More than 350 different species exist, with countless additional strains and varieties. In the 150 years since Louis Pasteur discovered that yeast fermentation produces carbon dioxide, which leavens dough, yeasts have been studied by every conceivable technology and harnessed to perform hundreds of different tasks, from cleaning up oil slicks to producing antibiotics. Many are artificially produced for very specific functions, including commercial bread making.

It is important to understand the basic differences between the wild yeasts of sourdough and the commercial baker's yeast used in most other breads. First, sourdough yeasts grow best in acidic doughs, while baker's yeast does better in neutral or slightly alkaline doughs. Baker's yeast is a single species, *Saccharomyces cerevisiae,* with hundreds of strains and varieties, while sourdoughs are usually leavened by one or more species in the same dough, none of which is baker's yeast. Baker's yeast is a highly uniform product that produces an equally uniform texture in bread dough. The wild yeasts are anything but uniform, and they vary from country to country. But the most impressive difference between the two yeast types is that a single package of instant dried yeast produces just one batch of bread, while the same amount of wild sourdough culture produces loaf after loaf for the lifetimes of many bakers.

In one gram of commercial cake yeast there are twenty to twenty-four billion individual yeast cells; in a package of dry yeast there are 130 billion. By comparison, a cup of sourdough culture as it comes from the refrigerator contains far fewer cells. This book emphasizes repeatedly that you should never use baker's yeast either in your sourdough culture or in the recipe of your sourdough bread. The addition of baker's yeast to a culture may overwhelm the wild yeast and destroy the culture. In addition, you risk the introduction of a bacteriophage, or virus, to which the commercial cells are immune but that may kill wild yeast. Plus, if you leave your dough with baker's yeast, the open-texture characteristic of sourdough may disappear. The primary secret of sourdough success lies in the art of stimulating that wild culture, just before you use it in baking, into a burst of activity to equal the number of yeast cells found in commercial yeast. The steps of preparing the culture described in Chapter 3 do just that!

Research into Wild Sourdough Cultures

Bakers of every sort welcomed the introduction of commercial yeast in the late 1800s. It greatly simplified the baking process and made it much faster. But something happened to the sourdough flavor. It disappeared! In due time, researchers identified the problem. They found that sourdough bread is the product of not one microorganism but two: Wild yeasts make it rise and beneficial bacteria provide the flavor. These bacteria are primarily lactobacilli, so named because they produce lactic acid, which contributes to the sour flavor. They don't do it very fast. It requires approximately twelve hours for the bacteria to develop fully the authentic taste of sourdough, depending on the temperature of the dough. Extremely fast commercial yeasts, particularly active dry yeast, have shortened the rising process to two hours or less, giving the lactobacilli little chance to get started.

Lactobacilli produce the flavor of sourdough breads by fermentation, which is the primary reason why sourdoughs are completely different from, and better than, most commercial breads. Fermentation is that process by which a variety of bacterial organisms act on food products to produce different flavors, textures, and aromas. Examples include the fermentation of milk to produce cheese, yogurt, sour cream, and buttermilk. Many types of sausage involve fermentation of various meats. Fermentation is also essential in the production of various vegetable preparations, including pickles, sauerkraut, olives, and a host of dishes common in Europe and the Middle East. Finally, of course, wine and beer are made through the process of fermentation. But few of us are aware that fermentation is essential to the flavor of sourdoughs. Without sufficient time for that process to occur, the flavor will be lost.

Lactobacilli that produce the famous taste of San Francisco sourdough have been studied by Leo Kline and T. F. Sugihara, two food scientists working at the Western Regional Laboratory of the Department of Agriculture in Albany, California. They determined that many bakeries in the area were using sourdough colonized by identical strains of yeast and lactobacilli. The widespread occurrence of these organisms was not because the bakeries shared their starters with one another, but because these organisms are dominant throughout the San Francisco area. This led them to name this strain of bacteria *Lactobacillus sanfrancisco*. In 1970 and 1971, they published the results of their studies on San Francisco sourdough in *The Bakers Digest* and *Applied Microbiology*.

Kline and Sugihara identified for the first time the wild yeast *Torulopsis holmii*, later reclassified as *Candida milleri*, now as *Candida humilis*, as the lactobacilli responsible for the sourdough process and provided instructions for producing it. The yeasts also have a common and unusual characteristic: They are unable to utilize maltose, one of the carbohydrates found in flour. This assumes special significance since the lactobacilli require the maltose unused by the yeast, thereby establishing a symbiosis between the two organisms. Further evidence indicates that the lactobacilli produce an antibiotic that protects the culture from contamination by harmful bacteria. This strong mutual dependence is thought to be responsible for the survival of the culture in San Francisco bakeries for over one hundred years. It also explains why the culture successfully resists contamination when used in other areas. In 1973, Kline and Sugihara applied for and received a patent based on those studies. This statement appears in that patent: "One of the objects of the invention is to provide the means whereby the unique product (San Francisco sourdough) can be manufactured efficiently, economically and in any location regardless of climate or topography." To this day, contrary to that statement, I continue to hear from bakers who doubt that the San Francisco culture will function outside the San Francisco area.

The work of Kline and Sugihara was intended for use by commercial bakers, but with modifications it is extremely helpful to home bakers as well. When the research was being done, San Francisco bakers "rebuilt" the starter every eight hours, several days a week. Current methods suggest that timing was more an accommodation to the workday than to the needs of the culture. When starters were rebuilt, 25 to 40 percent of the previous starter was used to rebuild the new one. This provided a massive inoculum of the microorganisms and a very acidic environment that helped prevent contamination by other organisms. When the starter was used in the bread recipe, however, it represented only 11 percent of the total mix, while methods in many artisan bakeries today use as much as 40 percent. The starter sponge was made with high-gluten flour milled from Montana spring wheat containing 14 percent protein, while the recipe used a regular "patent" flour. Artisan bakers now often use all-purpose flour for both. After mixing, the starter was proofed for seven to eight hours at 75° to 80°. Once the loaves were formed, they received an additional proofing of six to eight hours at 85° to 90°. Artisan and home bakers now commonly proof longer at room temperature. It must be emphasized that Kline and Sugihara used a specific sourdough culture with the organisms they identified. Until 1998, artisan and home bakers were usually not able to acquire that culture.

Additional studies have looked at sourdoughs from Italy, the Middle East, India, Denmark, and Germany. Unlike most bacteria, lactobacilli thrive in the acid environment of sourdough and produce a variety of mild organic acids, alcohols, and countless additional compounds vital to the flavor of the doughs. One researcher has listed no fewer than fifty-five separate compounds in sourdoughs, many of them, of course, present only in trace amounts.

Research on bacteria that ferment bread is minuscule compared to the work on milk, meat, and vegetable fermentations. Although much of the research on other foods is not directly related to sourdoughs, many analogies are valuable in understanding the action of bacteria in bread doughs. Work on milk fermentation has identified a group of factors that inhibit the growth of starter bacteria in the production of cheese and yogurt. These include antibiotics present in the milk of cows that have been treated to prevent udder infections and in sanitizers used in cleaning milking machines. These findings point out the importance of never adding anything to your sourdough culture except flour and water. Further, if you experience inconsistent results with recipes calling for milk, inhibitors of this type may be involved.

Sourdough research in Germany and Denmark has also revealed the presence of different lactobacilli. Sourdough cultures appear to be colonized by the specific types of yeast and lactobacilli found where the cultures originate, explaining why breads from different areas often have distinctive characteristics. While directing the pathology department of a hospital laboratory in Saudi Arabia, I studied the microbiology of sourdough cultures my wife and I collected during our travels in the Middle East and Europe. Each contained a dominant yeast accompanied by several strains of lactobacilli. The wild yeast in each of the cultures revealed different physical characteristics under the microscope. I isolated both yeasts and bacteria in pure culture, then recombined them to test the combination after excluding interfering organisms. Detailed studies demonstrated that each culture represented a different yeast-lactobacillus combination of one wild yeast and two to four different lactobacilli strains. Our studies moved from the laboratory to home kitchens where thirty of our friends and associates tested the baking and taste differences.

They helped to confirm that, indeed, each culture, whether it was from Bahrain or Saudi Arabia or San Francisco, produced a different bread.

We wondered, could one of those cultures be the same combination that puzzled an Egyptian baker ten thousand years before? We felt, at times, close to that ancient Egyptian who first saw sourdough bubbles.

THE INGREDIENTS OF

Chapter 2

SOURDOUGH BREAD

F ew would argue with the statement that a good consistent culture, or starter, is the single most essential ingredient for sourdough success. Well, I am one of those few. The last eleven years have convinced me that one ingredient is of far more importance than any other. That ingredient is the baker wearing the apron. Successful sourdough baking demands the patience, skill, perseverance, and ingenuity of the baker.

Your Cultures

The second most essential ingredient is probably the culture. Most wild cultures are mixtures of several strains of wild yeast and lactobacilli. Some leaven rapidly, some quite slowly. Some leaven for extremely long proofing times, some not nearly so long. Some are very mild, others quite sour. Some have a subtle flavor independent of the degree of sourness.

You can beg, borrow, or steal a culture or you can buy a very good one from me at Sourdoughs International. Failing all that, you can rough it and capture your own by simply exposing a mixture of flour and water to the air. When the right organisms find your mixture, they will grow and thrive. For the most part, the wrong ones won't even like flour and water and thus won't thrive in it. So, create a mixture of 2 cups good-quality bread flour (see page 11) and 1½ cups warm water in a 2-quart plastic, glass, or stainless-steel bowl. Stir it with sufficient vigor to beat in additional air, then expose it to the air, preferably outdoors, although it can be done inside as well. Do not cover the bowl with plastic or anything else that will exclude the organisms you are attempting to capture. If insects or other critters are a potential problem, place cheesecloth or other fine mesh over the top. Stir the mixture vigorously at least twice every 24 hours. In 2 or 3 days, bubbles should appear on the surface as the first indication of success. Feed the culture an additional 1 cup flour and sufficient water to maintain the consistency and stir briskly again. You may need to repeat additional feeding at 6- to 12-hour intervals for several successive days.

When you capture a yeast that is sufficiently active to be useful, it will form a layer of foam 1 to 2 inches deep. If it doesn't attain this level of activity in 4 to 5 days, or begins to have a repulsive odor, you should abandon the attempt and repeat the process in a different location. There are no guarantees, and you may encounter problems with contamination, particularly in areas with heavy air pollution. Once you have a good, bubbly culture, transfer it to one or more widemouthed quart canning jars or similar containers and refrigerate it. Don't freeze it, as some strains of wild yeast won't survive freezing. Don't leave it on a warm kitchen counter for several days either, or the activity of the culture will make the mixture too acidic and inhibit the organisms.

You should be aware of some disagreement about the origin of sourdough organisms. Some believe they come from grain when it is milled into flour. As a result, some artisan bakers recommend using freshly ground organic flour in the mixture, and they cover the bowl with plastic to keep everything else out. Rye flours are an acknowledged source of the organisms of "rye sours," but I'm a bit skeptical about wheat flours. The term lactobacilli is misleading since lacto refers to milk, and the lactobacilli of sourdough use only flour as a nutrient. Apparently these strains were not recognized when the bacteria were named. Some years ago *Sunset* magazine ran a series of features extolling the use of yogurt as a source of sourdough lactobacilli. The problem, as I see it, is the baker was instructed to add milk to his starter to feed the yogurt bacteria. This is not the best idea, as milk occasionally contains antibiotics and disinfectant chemicals (see page 30) that may kill the organisms in the culture. In addition, the recipes called for baker's yeast to leaven the dough, which is also incompatible with my definition of traditional sourdough.

In the last few years, a French company has introduced a dried sourdough culture to the United States, marketing it to both commercial and home bakers. It has been described as a "dry mixture of specialized yeast, bacteria, and lactose" and is promoted as a starter that will produce an "assertive loaf." Among the ingredients listed on each packet is baker's yeast. Interestingly, the instruction material that accompanies the packet includes a bread recipe that lists even more "instant yeast" as an ingredient. The manufacturer says that each packet holds enough dried starter to produce twelve loaves, at which point the baker needs to purchase another packet. (The identical packets for the commercial baker contain instructions indicating the same amount will produce over one hundred loaves, and that a new packet is needed for each new batch of dough.) As you know, by my definition, such a product does not produce traditional sourdough.

You may think me a bit negative about collecting your own wild culture. That may be so, but it isn't because I'd like to sell you one. Remember, you have to catch two organisms, not one. While you can see convincing evidence of wild yeast in your mixture when the foam appears, that doesn't tell you much, if anything, about the presence or absence of good lactobacilli. That you can only judge when you taste the bread. But let me leave you with a bit of encouragement. Not long ago I received the following letter, which made my day. Perhaps it will do the same for you.

Dear Dr. Wood,

Somehow I was convinced to purchase your book from amazon.com. I wasn't specifically interested in sourdough. My husband had tried a recipe once . . . that was a mess! I would hate to tell you of the years of bad bread making I have had.

I decided to try, with the curiosity of a mad scientist, to capture the wild yeast just outside my front door. This was a strange concept. I had always thought that yeast was something made in a chemical lab somewhere out of beer. To find that for all of these years I've been hoodwinked. This must change!

My husband and I discussed the idea. New Jersey was probably too polluted to have wild yeast. It probably wouldn't work and if it did work it would probably be something mutated (a genetic monster). Given New Jersey's nickname "New York's landfill," we were skeptical. I decided to try anyway. I set out the flour and water mixture and placed a steamer upside down to keep the varmints away. After three days bubbles appeared. I was inspired! I fed the culture at 12-hour intervals and waited a week for foam. I got a tiny bit of foam around the bubbles, but nothing like what the book had indicated. Another week went by. By now I needed two containers, but I kept hoping that the starter would foam! Then I thought about changing location. I brought one inside and set it on the dining room table. The other I left outside. I fed both, and let them sit. As you probably have already guessed, the inside culture exploded with foam all over my dining room table and tried to make a break for it on my floor. The other hadn't changed. I was ecstatic!

I made the World Bread and some Cinnamon Rolls. The loaves didn't keep their shape but I baked them anyway. Light and fluffy . . . yum. The cinnamon rolls were big and fat. My days of buying yeast are over. I'm having a world of fun. I'm going to try to use it in some of my other recipes. My husband is still a skeptic—New Jersey yeast must glow in the dark or something. Wish me luck!

Lois, in Parlin, New Jersey

The moral of this story: You don't need to buy a culture from anyone. But you can see with letters like this why I've still got a warm glow.

Flour

Wheat Bread Flour

Plant geneticists have produced a large number of wheat varieties designed for highly specific conditions and purposes, including soil type, growing temperatures, average rainfall, protein content, disease resistance, harvesting characteristics, yields per acre, and even adaptability to commercial automated bread machines. These bread-flour varieties fall into four major categories: hard and soft winter wheat and hard and soft spring wheat. Hard wheat has a "strong" gluten, which is required to trap the leavening gases and to form and maintain the shape of the loaf. Soft wheat has a "weak" gluten and is used to make various pastries, crackers, and similar products.

Spring wheat is planted in spring and harvested in late summer. It is grown primarily in Montana, the Dakotas, Minnesota, and Canada, since the winters are often too cold in these areas for the wheat planted in the fall to survive. It is known throughout the world as Manitoba or dark northern spring wheat and is considered to be the hardest wheat produced. Winter wheat is planted in the fall, lies dormant over the winter, and is harvested in early summer.

The milling method, that is, the grinding and sifting process that produces flour from grain kernels, is an additional variable. During milling, the components of the kernel are separated depending on the type of flour being produced. The largest portion of a wheat kernel is the endosperm, which contains about 75 percent of the kernel's protein and is the source of white flour. Bran is the outer coating of the kernel and is included in whole-wheat flour. The embryo or sprouting section of the seed is the germ. It contains fats and oils and is usually separated from flours since it becomes rancid during long storage.

In ancient times, milling was done between two heavy stones that not only removed the kernel's husk, but also ground the remaining portions so finely that they could not be separated. Some modern milling techniques still use special millstones, but the degree of fineness can now be regulated and the kernel components can be separated. Some believe that stone grinding is done primarily for its promotional value but there is evidence that the process, which is cooler than steel rollers, produces a different and more nutritional flour. These flours are highly touted to home bakers, but today nearly all flour in the United States is milled by high-speed steel rollers.

White flour is available in two major categories. Bleached flours are treated with chlorine compounds or other bleaching agents to whiten them. They may also be treated with a number of chemical additives to improve baking characteristics. Unbleached flours generally have no chemical additives. Both are usually enriched with several of the B vitamins, iron, and folic acid.

High-protein unbleached flours can be produced from hard spring wheats with strong gluten that need no additives to improve their performance. Lower-quality flours are often treated with oxidizing agents to strengthen their gluten. They may be blended with several other flour types and may even include barley. All-purpose flours fall into this group.

Whole-wheat flours contain most of the components of the wheat kernel and are more nutritious than white flours. Enrichment standards established by the FDA in the early 1940s for white flours have narrowed the nutritional differences between the two flour types; however, whole wheat generally contains part or all of the wheat germ and will become rancid unless stored in the refrigerator or freezer. Most whole wheat is milled from selected hard spring wheat, making it an excellent product for the sourdough baker. It is available in a variety of grinds, from very fine to very coarse. Cracked wheat is cut rather than ground and is used in bread recipes for special texture and flavor. Flaked and rolled wheats are also available.

Unfortunately, flour labels rarely list whether the wheat is hard or soft, winter or spring. Most flours are a mixture of wheats, but the types and proportions remain a mystery, or perhaps even a secret. These blends are ostensibly made to improve baking performance. It would appear they could also be used to upgrade and utilize lesser flours. Grinding your own wheat is one way—perhaps the only way—to guarantee the type and quality of your flour and may offer a source of satisfaction as well. Home grinding machines usually are incapable of separating the kernel components, however, and thus produce only whole-wheat flours.

The sourdough baker needs flour with a high protein content and strong gluten, making hard spring wheat ideal. For better than three decades, I believed every word of that statement. But then, while preparing a feature about sourdoughs for *Organic Gardening,* I was queried by the editor as to why I was advising readers to use flour with strong gluten. At first blush, I was hard-pressed to define a specific reason. After all, a strong flour gluten has long been understood by everyone to be better for making bread than a weak gluten flour. But the question forced me into some research, and I found that cereal chemists are experts at concealing what they don't know. They are quick to declare that there are two clearly defined types, strong (hard wheat) and weak (soft wheat), but they admit that there are no differences in the amino acid profiles of the two flours. From there they deviate into two major gluten components, the gliadins and glutenins. The latter, with a higher molecular weight, are thought to be responsible for the "viscoelastic" properties of dough. And it has been observed that weak flours have glutens that stretch easily, while glutens of strong flours are more compact and more resistant to rapid stretching. The answers seemed too complex for the article I was writing, and perhaps for these pages as well. But what I discovered would come back to haunt me.

This story begins in the Boise Co-op, where I found myself with too much time to kill and started looking at flours in the bulk foods section. The names left me mildly skeptical and a little curious. As usual there wasn't a clue about source or content on any of the flour bins. My first impression was anything but positive, and I suspected they were probably ground from cheaper grades of soft wheat. Anyway, I left with about five pounds each of three varieties modestly labeled Unbleached Peak Performance, Ultimate Performance, and Premium Flour. I was hatching a plan, so to round out my collection I also bought some King Arthur All-Purpose Flour, described on the package as "milled from hard winter wheat with no soft wheat." I already had some General Mills Gold Medal Better for Bread and some Joseph's Best All-Purpose Organic Flour from Certified Foods. The only visible difference among the six flours was price, with Peak Performance the least expensive at thirty-nine cents per pound and King Arthur's All-Purpose the most expensive at sixty-six cents per pound in a five-pound package.

So I had six flours to test-bake from various sources and not much information about any of them except price. The test recipe included ½ cup Original San Francisco culture, 4½ cups "test" flour, 1½ cups water, and 1½ teaspoons salt. I mixed and kneaded each dough in the same way and made rounds that I proofed overnight at room temperature. The following day, after approximately 16 hours of proofing, I punched down the doughs and formed pan loaves, which then proofed an additional 4 hours, for a total of 20 hours, until they were ready for baking.

So what happened? In spite of my bias, the doughs all demonstrated good to excellent rises and all produced reasonable to excellent sourdough breads. The best rises (volumes) occurred with the Peak Performance and Ultimate Performance. The smallest volumes were seen with the Premium and King Arthur All-Purpose. The best sourdough texture characterized, in part, as the largest, irregular holes, was produced by Joseph's Best All-Purpose Organic and the Premium Flours. The Gold Medal and King Arthur's flours resulted in the least desirable texture, that is, small uniform holes. The sourdough flavor and sourness were good to excellent with all six flours.

A week later, I made another trip to the Boise Co-op and found out that Peak Performance came from Guisto's Vita Grain in San Francisco and was milled from hard red wheat. The Premium Flour was from Camas Grain in the area of Fairfield, Idaho (known primarily for its soft white wheat), and the label indicated it was a wheat flour plus enzymes for improved baking. The Ultimate was described as organic but had no ingredient information. I also became aware of another bulk flour, Red Rose from the Central Milling in Logan, Utah. Priced at twenty-five cents per pound, it was described as a best-seller, possibly as a result of price.

I couldn't resist one more baking trial to compare the inexpensive Red Rose with two flours said to be from hard red wheat, Peak Performance and King Arthur's All-Purpose. As before I made up the three test doughs, using the same mixing and kneading techniques, but instead of making them into rounds for additional proofing, I formed two loaves from each dough. I proofed one loaf of each pair at 85° and the other at room temperature (68°). After five hours at 85°, the three loaves were virtually identical and ready to bake. But at room temperature it took the loaves ten hours to reach the same stage, and they were quite different. The least expensive, Red Rose, flour produced the best volume and the best texture. The King Arthur flour was second in volume but rated last in texture. Peak Performance was last in volume, second in texture. All three flours, however, produced acceptable sourdough breads in texture and flavor.

I used to believe bulk foods represented a bargain, and I have always believed Gold Medal was overpriced. As these words were written, Gold Medal was selling at twenty-eight cents per pound in a twenty-five-pound bag. So much for bargains in bulk flours. A week after I wrote these words, Gold Medal was on sale and twenty-five pounds were priced at $4.48 or eighteen cents per pound. So I bought a hundred pounds and ate my words.

Is there a message in all this? I think so. For sourdoughs, within limits, it really doesn't matter if you're using a high-quality flour or not. To begin with, the concept of flour quality is tenuous indeed. Even the so-called experts agree that flour quality and flour strength remain difficult to define. Ironically, the best method to determine baking quality and strength of a flour remains a baking test, and this is certainly true for sourdoughs. If a weak flour stretches more easily than a strong flour, it may very well produce the open structure with large irregular spaces so important to the texture of a traditional sourdough. One can only wonder why strong wheat became so popular in the first place. When you realize, however, that uniformity and consistency of bread texture is a high priority of the commercial baker, it suggests where the concept originated.

Old cookbooks advise buying flour near where the wheat was produced to assure flour of a specific quality. That is hardly practical today. Wheat is shipped and traded all over the world. The urban dweller is clearly at the mercy of the local supermarket. In the final analysis, one must depend on reliable brand names and experiment with various types of flour. So when you find a flour that works for you, stay with it until it changes, which may be as soon as the next growing season.

One closing caution: Avoid self-rising flours or instant flours, which contain dried yeasts or chemical leaveners or both. In general, 1 cup self-rising flour contains 1½ teaspoons leavening agent and ½ teaspoon of salt.

Organic Flour

Organic wheat flours are becoming more widely available in bulk food sections and health food stores. If organic foods are important to you for health or even moral reasons, you can bake organic sourdoughs more cheaply than you can buy them. Although the big flour companies and commercial bakeries are testing the organic waters, the process of organic certification is time-consuming and expensive. But it is coming.

Steve Curran, with the help of several co-ops in Nebraska and Colorado, established Rocky Mountain Flour Milling in 1997. He invented the special equipment that produces nothing but certified organic flour in Platteville, Colorado, with a capacity to produce one hundred thousand pounds per twenty-four hours. Joseph Vanderliet operates a stone milling company, Certified Foods, in San Leandro, California. Joe spent two days with me last summer getting acquainted with sourdoughs and educating me about Certified Foods. He left me with ten pounds of Joseph's Best All-Purpose Organic Flour, and I am well on the way to becoming a convert. I introduced one of my jars of Original San Francisco culture to a diet of Joe's organic flour, and it has done just fine. I have baked successfully with it several times.

I have no intention of selling a certified organic sourdough culture, however. The National Organic Standards Board says, among five hundred other things, that to be labeled "organic," 95 percent of the ingredients in a product must be organically produced. Alas, the hassles and record keeping of certification do not fit my lifestyle. But I will tell you how I made my culture, and you can make your own. Start with any culture you like, dump out everything but 1 cup, then feed it with 1 cup organic white flour and sufficient water to maintain the original consistency. Proof until active, then repeat the whole process about ten times over a couple of weeks. At that point, your organic culture will be very happy, with far less than 5 percent of anything other than organic food.

Durum Flour

Just about every baking book that describes flours will tell you there are three major kinds, wheat, rye, and durum. Wheat and rye, they say, are bread flours, but durum is used for pastas. Don't you believe it. In many Middle Eastern countries, durum has long been the primary bread flour. In Italy, bread making started as a family chore and is still a tradition in many parts of the country. Durum is a major ingredient and the breads are largely made with natural leavens.

I, too, had thought durum was used almost exclusively to produce pastas and that it was a soft wheat. That was before I became acquainted with Arlen Gilbertson, a durum farmer near Parshall in North Dakota. He farms several hundred acres of durum, and we became lifelong friends when he and one of his sons helped me remove hundreds of porcupine quills from my hapless Brittany. We had lots of opportunity to talk during that hours-long process. I can still remember him holding a kernel of durum between his fingers and pointing out that it was almost translucent. Then he tapped it with a hammer demonstrating its hardness. It is a spring wheat and, when he told me the protein content was between 14 and 17 percent, I wondered why no one was making bread with it. He wasn't sure, but I left with a sack of Arlen's durum and Dr. Elias's phone number.

Dr. Elias is an assistant professor in the Department of Plant Sciences at North Dakota State University. Born in Syria, he is, not surprisingly, very familiar with durum in bread. He explained to me that not all glutens are alike, and that durum wheats and their glutens have been selected specifically to produce the qualities in pastas that have made North Dakota durums famous worldwide. He also described an ongoing research program at the university to develop durums with better-quality glutens. I suspect, however, that the research remains oriented toward better glutens for pastas. Dr. Elias sent me data on four new varieties named Renville, Monroe, Vic, and Munich, all having improved glutens over former strains.

A version of these comments appeared in *World Sourdoughs from Antiquity*, which prompted many inquiries from home bakers on sources of the better durums. I have referred everyone back to Dr. Elias, and he is probably wishing he had never talked to me. So, here are a couple of new possibilities for durums. I know Arlen Gilbertson is growing Renville and possibly some of the other new varieties. He is not in the mail-order business, but I will pass along a sneaky idea. He and his wife, Ronna, have recently opened a delightful bed and breakfast just above Deep Water Bay on Lake Sakakawea. If you want to stop by and have some great walleye fishing at the same time, you can probably come away with a sack of durum. Their web site is www.jwp.bc.ca/deepwater/. The other possibility is Joe Vanderliet at Certified Foods (see Selected Sources). With luck, he will eventually get into the mail-order business for flours in small quantities.

Kamut Flour

Kamut has an intriguing history shrouded in controversy that hasn't diminished over the years. In the 1940s, a serviceman stationed in Portugal was given a few grains of wheat said to be from King Tut's tomb. In time, that grain found its way to the Quinn ranch in Montana, where it was planted and produced organically for a number of years. In the 1980s, Bob Quinn studied the grain, classified it as *Triticum polonicum*, and named it kamut, an Egyptian word for wheat. Quinn believes it is unlikely that the grain could have survived to germinate in King Tut's tomb, but he says it may represent an isolated strain of ancient wheat perhaps still grown in small cultivars in Egypt. The grain is closely related to emmer, the great-grandfather of modern wheats, but unlike emmer, kamut threshes free of its hull, making it a so-called naked wheat like all modern wheats. Quinn continues to produce the grain organically on his Montana ranch but now markets it primarily through Arrowhead Mills in Texas and other outlets. It is widely available in nutrition and health food stores. It imparts a distinctive nutty flavor to sourdough bread.

On a trip with the National Geographic Society in 1993, I took along quite a bit of kamut. It seemed appropriate considering the journey's purpose was to rediscover how the Egyptians baked man's first bread, an exploration later reported on in *National Geographic* magazine. While in Egypt, I spent an afternoon at an old agricultural museum. The grain exhibits were housed in glass cases that were sometimes almost totally obscured by dust. Some critics of Quinn's taxonomy have cast doubt that kamut ever occurred in Egypt, so I was delighted to see one case containing a sheaf of grain labeled *Triticum polonicum* from a remote Egyptian site. Perhaps more provocative was an exhibit labeled *T. pyramidalis,* a grain I had never heard of but that certainly has a King Tut ring to it.

Spelt Flour

Spelt may be even more ancient than kamut, as it is said by some to have originated more than nine thousand years ago. It has been popular in Europe for thousands of years and today is carried by many European food stores. It has a tough husk that is difficult to remove, requiring special dehusking equipment. Amish farmers in Ohio introduced it to the United States, but they primarily fed it to livestock. In the 1980s Wilhelm Kosnopfl, then president of Purity Foods, financed a spelt research program at Ohio University and subsequently developed a facility at Okemos, Michigan, to provide spelt products to health food stores. In a conversation with Willy Kosnopfl early in 1996, he commented, "In Europe, spelt is used almost exclusively with sourdoughs." We both speculated that there may be something intrinsic about sourdough fermentation that makes it particularly well adapted to spelt flours and vice versa.

The original marketing of spelt was a bit flamboyant, describing it as a nonwheat grain and therefore ideal for gluten-sensitive individuals. Most agronomists would disagree and consider spelt to be a distinct species of wheat. There is little general agreement on its allergenic properties. Nonetheless, spelt is a remarkable grain that produces terrific sourdough breads. The flour turns out a soft, satiny dough with minimal kneading. Various research studies seem to indicate that spelt gluten degrades rapidly during mixing, suggesting that mixing times should be limited for best results. Kneading does not appear to be affected, however, according to Don Stinchcomb, current president of Purity Foods.

Most of my test baking is with sourdough cultures grown in a mixture of white bread flour and water. For testing spelt flours, I fed a Russian culture a diet of spelt flours until I was confident it was almost entirely composed of spelt. The results were impressive. The culture itself had an entirely different texture, almost like thick whipped cream. I baked recipes using 100 percent white spelt flour and mixtures of up to 68 percent whole spelt flour. The loaves uniformly leavened as well as doughs made with the same recipe using 100 percent white bread flour. I compared kneading for five minutes and ten minutes and could detect no difference.

The product I evaluated is called Vita-Spelt and is produced by Purity Foods. It is advertised as organic, unenriched, unbleached, and unbromated and has produced exquisite sourdoughs. I have included several recipes for you to enjoy.

If you want to make sourdough bread with 100 percent spelt, it is easy to transfer your culture from bread flour to a total spelt flour base. It you are activating a dried culture, simply substitute white spelt flour for white bread flour. If you already have an activated bread flour culture, put ¼ cup into a quart canning jar, add 1 cup warm water, stir vigorously, and add 1 cup white spelt flour. Stir briefly and proof at 85° for approximately 12 hours. Then take ¼ cup of this culture and repeat the process. After four or five repetitions you will have diluted the bread flour to an insignificant level.

Rye Flour

Rye is grown mainly in the Dakotas, Minnesota, and Nebraska, in soils requiring hardy grain varieties. It is a winter grain, planted in the fall and harvested the following summer. Rye flour has limited gluten content, and breads made entirely with it do not rise well. It is usually mixed with wheat flour to produce a lighter loaf with rye flavor. Sourdough cultures originating in central Europe, where rye has been a dominant grain for centuries, may be better adapted to fermenting rye doughs.

When rye is milled, two basic types of flour are produced, white and dark. White rye flour is made only from the endosperm. It is particularly recommended for mildly flavored Jewish and other light rye breads. It is generally mixed with 60 to 70 percent good-quality white flour. Dark rye is a more distinctive-flavored dark flour used in heavy, dark rye breads such as German,

Swedish, and pumpernickel. It is usually mixed with about 80 percent high-protein white flour or whole-wheat flour. Pumpernickel is a coarse dark rye flour made by grinding the entire rye kernel. It is analogous to whole wheat and is milled in fine, medium, and coarse grinds. Rye blends are also available that combine regular or dark rye with a good-quality high protein white flour.

Wheat Gluten

Arrowhead Mills produces a product called Vital Gluten that is useful for increasing the leavening potential of gluten-deficient flours such as the rye varieties. Other mills sell a similar product simply labeled "gluten flour." Gluten is extracted from wheat flour through a water-washing procedure, yielding a fine, white concentrated product. Arrowhead recommends 1½ teaspoons per cup for whole-grain breads. It is especially useful in bread machines if insufficient leavening is a problem.

Flax

In 1998, Lydia, one of our newsletter readers, penned us a note describing a particular offering at a Canadian conference on nutrition. In the note she stated: "The subject for one of the days was 'flax seed' and the tremendous benefits of the omega-3 fatty acids that flax contains. With today's emphasis on heart-healthy foods, it was indeed very heartening to be able to obtain something that tastes so good and is so cheap to buy. I am a fan of flaxseed and have a printout of its nutritional qualities that I have obtained from [Pizzey's Milling and Baking Company in Manitoba], Box 132, Angusville, R0J 0A0 Manitoba . . . . You might want to experiment with flax and sourdough. There are no recipes in your book using flaxseed or milled flax. I have been very successful using it with both commercial yeast and sourdough."

Her timing was perfect. I became acquainted with Linda Pizzey over the telephone, and she was delighted to send some samples of milled flax and whole flaxseed for bake tests with sourdoughs. But *our* timing was awful. It was the middle of a UPS strike, and it would be several weeks before the order arrived. In the meantime, I had become intrigued with seeing the great concentrations of snow geese in the Canadian Provinces as they "stage" for their fall migration flights to the southern United States and Mexico. It seemed like a great opportunity for a quick trip to Manitoba to see the beginning of the world's greatest migration and to visit the Pizzey Mill at Angusville, so my wife and I loaded our camper and took off for Manitoba. It took three days to reach the border on Highway 83 south of Melita, where we got directions to Whitewater Lake. We were a little early for the peak migration, so only about fifty thousand geese were in the immediate area, but that was enough for an unbelievable sight. The noise from that many birds talking and flying drowns out any attempt at conversation.

After two days with geese blackening the sky, we headed north toward Angusville. We didn't know what to expect at the Pizzey Mill. The letterhead describes the operation as "A Farm-Based Milling and Baking Company." Over the telephone Linda had drawn a verbal map that terminated after a little less than two miles on a graveled road. We had driven over a thousand miles, and now we were traveling through an area of grainfields separated by generous wood lots. Suddenly the Pizzey Mill appeared on the horizon. We were instantly impressed with the number of tall grain silos and supporting buildings. Above the rooftops, in a brisk wind, flew the Canadian and Manitoban flags.

As we approached an administration office we encountered a worker dressed in coveralls operating a boom structure that was transferring grain from a large truck to one of the silos. That worker was Glenn Pizzey, owner and operator of the Pizzey Mill. Glenn and Linda are the quintessence of the entrepreneurial spirit. Glenn graduated from the University of Manitoba with a degree in agriculture. Since then, he and Linda have been promoting a flax dream. He laughs as he describes the reaction of his neighbors to his coming home from school, selling his cows, plowing up his wheat fields, and planting flax. Today, along with Linda and half a dozen employees, he runs a very impressive business. When asked how he picked that particular site, he tells the story of his great grandparents from England who rode the new railroad to the end of the line and were dumped off with all their possessions to make it on their own. In that area he built his mill 150 years later, still pioneering as had his grandparents.

The Pizzeys operate a different kind of mill. While flax is their specialty, they mill, process, package, market, and distribute many other grain products as well. On the same day that they ship several giant containers to Denmark or Australia, they also package grains, flax, and baking mixes in two- to twenty-five-pound packages for the home consumer, which they market directly by mail order or through distributors to food outlets. Most of the big U.S. mills ship only to large industrial outlets, but not the Pizzeys!

When we returned from Manitoba, I did a number of bake tests to determine how flax would perform with sourdoughs. On many occasions I have noted that the fermentation of sourdoughs improves the baking characteristics of various flours, and I was curious to see if that would occur with flax. In the first tests I used it as an ingredient in recipes, which resulted in only about two hours of fermentation. Later I did two tests doubling the amount of flax. In another I used it as a partial substitute for some of the flour. All of the loaves leavened exceptionally well. I cut a still-hot loaf from one of the first tests and thought it excellent and different, with an unusual whole-grain flavor. The next day I tried a loaf from the recipe with twice as much flax flour. The flavor was distinctive and delicious.

The Flax Council of Canada puts out an information packet on Canadian flax that includes a free cookbook with a dozen bread recipes using flax by both conventional and bread-machine methods. You can contact them at 465-167 Lombard Ave., Winnipeg, MB R3B 0T6, Canada. Phone (204) 982-2115; fax (204) 942-1841; e-mail flax@flaxcouncil.ca or visit their web site at www.flaxcouncil.ca.

The message in all this is simple. Flax, the new barleys, special fibers, durum, and so on all make health claims of one sort or another. That is not necessarily the best reason to change your diet to include them. However, they all add something special to the flavor and texture of sourdough breads, and they just may increase your longevity. One thing is certain. You can enjoy the omega-3 of flax for a lot lower cost than the omega-3 of salmon.

Bulgur

I vaguely remembered hearing about bulgur in the early 1960s, when it was being touted as a solution to feeding starving millions in various underdeveloped countries. After that, it more or less dropped out of sight. Then, in the June 1999 Technical Bulletin from the American Institute of Baking, bulgur was pronounced a gourmet food in the United States, one that was becoming a primary ingredient in dishes on many restaurant and deli menus. This starring role was news to me. But what I found most intriguing was the use of bulgur four thousand years ago. What could be more interesting than a sourdough baked with an ingredient that old? The bulletin was written by Michael Orlando, president of Sunnyland Mills in Fresno, California. I called him and we had a long and interesting conversation.

Bulgur is not a special variety of wheat. It is almost any wheat prepared by a special method that was apparently developed accidentally while in pursuit of long-term preservation. It is theorized that ancient civilizations boiled wheat kernels and then sun-dried them. The process produced a different and desirable flavor, and the grain was more resistant to mold contamination. More recently it has been discovered that the process also shifts desirable vitamins and minerals from the outer layers of the seed to the endosperm, the primary constituent of white flour, thus enriching it.

I had never heard of using bulgur in any bread, let alone sourdough. Orlando told me their bulgur is produced by cleaning, cooking, drying, grinding, and sifting special varieties of soft white wheat grown primarily in Washington, Oregon, and Idaho. I explained my interest in doing some sourdough bake tests with it, and within the week five samples of Sunnyland's various bulgur grades were delivered to my door.

As you will read later, the relative amounts of flour and water are very important in determining dough consistency. I usually strive to make a dough that is about 63 percent flour and 37 percent water, and I intended to incorporate the bulgur at the rate of about 20 percent of the total flour. None of the five samples had the fine consistency of flour, however, being composed of rather hard irregular particles produced by the grinding process. I instead decided to add the bulgur like any other nonflour ingredient. I hoped the fermentation process would soften the hard particles and maybe convert them to something special in flavor and texture.

I wasn't at all prepared for what happened. The results were dramatic. The dried bulgur slurped up water like it had just come in from the desert. My carefully planned recipes designed for 63 percent flour and 37 percent water went right out the window. I cut back on the amount of flour, but the doughs were still heavy and soggy. I proofed them overnight at room temperature and, to my surprise, they almost doubled in volume, but they were still leaden and stiff. They looked and felt more like Polish sausage than bread dough. With little optimism, I transferred them to a proofing box at 85°, hoping the warmer temperature might bring forth a miracle. I was planning to leave them for eight hours, but paused at the box two hours later to take a peek and confirm my failed experiment. In fifty years of baking, I have not been more surprised! In two hours the loaves had exploded upward and were almost an inch above the pan tops, ready to bake.

I baked them at 375° for forty minutes and noted a distinctly different aroma than I usually associate with sourdoughs. It was very pleasant but difficult to describe, perhaps a little alcoholic. The flavor, however, was delicious and unusual. Although some combination of the moisture in the dough and/or the fermentation process had softened the bulgur particles, I couldn't envision the hard whole-grain kernels ever being a reasonable ingredient in bread dough. I continued my experiments with both raw and cooked whole-grain bulgur. The bulgur kernels, either way, were nearly the same: firm but chewable and, although different, a perfect combination with sourdough.

And now more good news: As home bakers know, most specialty grains are produced and marketed for commercial bakeries and shipped in about twenty-ton lots. That's a little tough for us to use up in one lifetime and most of these products are hard to find in small quantities. Not so with bulgur. Michael Orlando tells me that almost 98 percent of bulk bulgur in health food and nutrition stores comes from Sunnyland Mills. He cautions the home baker to look for light-colored bulgur as opposed to dark brown. The latter is produced from hard red wheats, doesn't hydrate as well as the light bulgurs made from soft white wheats, and may have a slightly bitter taste.

Soy Products

My story of soy starts fifty years ago with a pioneer scientist who added three simple supplements to improve the nutritional quality of bread a hundredfold. Over the years many friends have urged me to extol the health benefits of sourdoughs as a way to get more home bakers involved. Until 1998 I had declined, feeling that the charisma and pleasure of traditional baking was more than sufficient to attract a crowd, and I don't like bogus health claims. But a chance occurrence altered my course.

In 1949, when I still believed anyone could change the world, I met a man who changed mine. Dr. Clive McCay was a professor of animal nutrition at Cornell University where I had enrolled in graduate school to study fishery biology. It was at a time when extensive research was being conducted on the nutritional requirements of fish to support the operation of massive salmon hatcheries on the Columbia River. McCay was a leader in that research and became an important mentor in my fishery studies, which involved the protein requirements of salmonids. When I left Cornell three years later for a position in a fishery research laboratory on the Columbia, I carried McCay's indelible mark, and I still do today.

In the years that followed, our paths didn't cross until I stumbled across *The Cornell Bread Book* by Clive and Jeanette McCay, first published in 1955. (A number of subsequent revisions have been published, the latest by Dover Publications in 1980. The occasional references that follow are by permission of Dover.) The Cornell bread was dubbed the *"Do-Good Loaf"* by Jean Hewitt in the *New York Times Sunday Magazine* and was reprinted among the *Times'* most requested recipes in 1972. Incidentally that publication of fifty-four recipes and McCay's cryptic comments is still available from Dover for $2.95. There is even a short section on sourdoughs that uses active dry yeast in every recipe. Well, no one is perfect, but that book is a fundamental classic that belongs in every baker's library.

"The thin rats always buried the fat ones." McCay's experiments showed that he could slow the growth and retard the onset of old-age diseases and death in rats by providing a reduced-calorie diet with plenty of vitamins, minerals, and proteins. His low-calorie diets often produced animals that lived twice as long.

When asked to improve the diet at New York State Mental Hospitals, he developed the Cornell bread formula, which was supplemented with soy flour, nonfat dry milk, and wheat germ. Soy flour is a rich protein concentrate with over 40 percent protein slightly deficient in methionine. When added to wheat flour, which has plenty of that amino acid but is deficient in the amino acid lysine, it produces a balanced protein comparable to meat. Nonfat dry milk supplies other amino acids that are deficient in wheat flours and is a good source of calcium. Wheat germ provides additional protein, iron, vitamin E, and B vitamins. When he did his research, the potential role of vitamin E in delaying or preventing Alzheimer's disease was unknown (and perhaps still is). When these three supplements were added to wheat flour, the breads (with butter) sustained McCay's rats through succeeding generations without additional food. Rats fed breads without the supplements died prematurely.

In their book the McCays describe methods for home bakers to produce their enriched breads by adding 1 tablespoon of soy flour, 1 tablespoon of nonfat dry milk, and 1 teaspoon of wheat germ for each cup of wheat flour. The book was written about two decades before the role of lactobacilli in producing the sourdough flavor was known, however, and the recipes all use baker's yeast, which has negligible lactobacilli. Dr. McCay died in 1967. Had he lived another twenty years, I have no doubt he would have used a wild sourdough to bake Cornell bread long before I did.

I knew our wild cultures could repeat Dr. McCay's work with a different and perhaps better flavor, and that his recipes would, in turn, make it a far more nutritional bread. I contacted the Protein Specialties Division of the Archer Daniels Midland Company (ADM), one of the world's largest soybean flour producers, and they sent me samples of many of their products. Included were Baker's Nutrisoy, a defatted flour that has been fully heat treated, and Soylect C-6 and C-15, which are Baker's Nutrisoy that has been refatted with 6 percent and 15 percent respectively soybean lecithin (a polyunsaturated fatty acid, the predominant source of choline, and one of the essential B vitamins). I found some full-fat soybean flour at the Boise Co-op and had everything I needed.

First, I combined 2 cups of our active Russian culture, ½ cup water, 1 tablespoon brown sugar, 1 teaspoon salt, 1 tablespoon vegetable oil, and 2½ cups bread flour. To this I added a mixture of 1½ tablespoons wheat germ, ¼ cup soy flour, and ½ cup nonfat dry milk. The results would have pleased Clive McCay. The control dough had no soy but an extra ¼ cup bread flour. The four breads, each with a different ADM soy flour or the Boise Co-op full-fat soy flour, rose exuberantly in 90 minutes and had excellent oven spring. The full-fat soy wasn't far behind. The texture and crumb of all were a little finer than most sourdoughs, producing a loaf that could be sliced thinner, if needed, for sandwich breads. The flavor, including the full-fat soy, was superb and distinctly different than the control.

So there you have it. Clive McCay said it this way: "All that any of us can do is to make the best use of available knowledge. We all appreciate that this is seldom done."

What is behind the increased interest in soys today? Historically, soybeans and soy flours have been used in the Orient since ancient times and as a substitute for wheat flours in the West for decades. Fifty years ago, the McCays recommended full-fat soy flour over defatted flours because of better appearance and quality. It is generally felt, however, that full-fat soys sometimes have an off flavor, and home bakers today usually prefer blander defatted flours. In addition, soybeans now are used in many different forms, including flours that are full fat, defatted, refatted, high enzyme, and grits. Also available are protein concentrates (containing at least 65 percent protein), protein isolates (at least 90 percent protein), and textured soy proteins (frequently made to resemble meat). Many of these products are formulated to improve their "functionality," which means they mix better with whatever they're added to as a supplement or perform better in a variety of mixing or processing equipment. Most are bland, a quality that tends to enhance the flavor of other foods.

The current interest in soys, however, in addition to the high protein content, is the presence of so-called phytonutrients. Specifically, soybeans are being recognized as an important source of phytoestrogens, which include the isoflavones, weak plant estrogens that occupy binding cites on reproductive cells where they inhibit overexposure to the body's natural estrogen and thus reduce breast cancer. They are also believed to play an important role in reducing menopausal symptoms and the risks connected with many chronic diseases of aging, including osteoporosis.

As I pursued additional information on soy isoflavones I became acquainted with Schouten USA, a major player in soy products and an independent division of the Royal Schouten Group, a 107-year-old Netherlands-based producer and marketer of raw materials and nutrients used by food industries throughout the world. In the mid-1990s, a Netherlands researcher developed a method of capturing isoflavones in soybeans and producing a natural concentrate now termed SoyLife. In 1995, Schouten USA began promoting SoyLife to the U.S. dietary supplement industry, with the result that more than two hundred products containing SoyLife are now available in health food stores.

Schouten sent me five pounds of the regular SoyLife complex, which the company describes as a "soy germ isoflavone concentrate." This particular batch contained 24.06 milligrams of isoflavones per gram of complex. The complex also comes in granules, a "micro" grind, and in a nongenetically modified (GMO) type.

My bake tests were designed to determine if the isoflavones would adversely affect the flavor and texture during the very long fermentation time of an authentic sourdough. I used our Original San Francisco culture, and the initial control recipe was ½ cup active culture, 6 cups bread flour, 2 cups water, and 1½ teaspoons salt. The test recipe was the same plus 0.56 ounces (on a postal scale) of isoflavone complex, resulting in a level equal to approximately 2 percent of the flour. Each recipe yielded two 1½-pound loaves.

The ingredients were mixed and kneaded to produce the dough, and a round was formed from each recipe. The rounds were lightly covered with plastic and proofed for 14 hours at room temperature (68°). After the initial proof, the doughs were lightly punched down and two pan loaves were formed from each batch. These were proofed for an additional 3 hours. At this point the four loaves were lightly floured and slashed. One control and one test loaf were then baked at 375° for 40 minutes. The remaining control and test loaf were refrigerated at 38° for an additional 11 hours and then baked.

The results showed the isoflavone complex had no effect on either the flavor or texture. Refrigerating the two loaves resulted in significantly more flavor and a better texture, with larger, more irregular holes and spaces.

So what does this mean? First, recognize that the isoflavone content was rather high. The recommended daily intake is in the range of 30 to 50 milligrams. In two loaves with a total of sixteen slices, the isoflavone content would be 23.6 milligrams per slice, or in twenty-four slices per two loaves, 15.7 milligrams. Thus, two slices of toast from either would supply most of the daily intake.

I sent a brief report on the bake tests to Schouten USA and took the opportunity to ask them about the availability of SoyLife complex in relatively small amounts for the home baker. It turns out their standard package is twenty kilograms (about forty-four pounds). In other words, you could repeat the above recipe about seventeen hundred times—more than most of us can handle. But that's not the end of the story. Schouten has expressed an interest in developing small packaging for home bakers, and you may see it sooner than you think in local health food stores.

In the meantime, take another long look at soy flours in general. You can find them in almost any health food or nutrition store. Full fat, defatted, and refatted with lecithin all make good sourdoughs. Keep in mind that the protein content of the best bread flour is about 14 percent. Most soy flours, by contrast, have a protein content of over 40 percent, and this is a protein that equals or betters that of wheat flour.

I need to acknowledge the efforts of a small, but determined, group to spread the word that soys have many detrimental nutritional characteristics. In my view, however, there are many more positives than negatives, but for contrary opinions, you can go to www.westonaprice.org.

Milk and Milk Products

Most commercially baked white breads in the United States are made with some form of milk, usually nonfat dried milk. In fact, the baking industry is the largest single consumer of this product in the country. Dried buttermilk, dried whole milk, and several whey products are also used in commercial breads. Any number of types of dried milk are available to home bakers, and you should experiment with them in your sourdoughs. Most of the recipes in this book that call for milk use 2 percent (low-fat) milk, but almost any milk or milk substitute is acceptable.

Remember, milk may contain antibiotics and trace amounts of disinfectants used to sterilize milking equipment. These contaminants may kill the organisms in your sourdough culture. Thus, do not use milk as a replacement for water in the culture.

Water

One seldom has control over one's source of water. Fortunately, water quality rarely poses a problem. Medium-hard water is perhaps best. Soft water is believed to result in sticky doughs that are difficult to handle. We have even used distilled water on occasion and found it difficult to detect any difference in dough consistency. Extremely alkaline water, however, will inhibit wild yeast activity and result in poor leavening. Contrary to considerable printed advice, trace metals usually have no deleterious effect, nor do fluoride additives. High iron concentrations also are of no consequence. One potential problem is chlorine. Chlorinated water has never been a problem in my baking, and I have encountered some pretty yucky stuff. But other bakers have reported problems that were solved by avoiding chlorine.

Salt

Salt has a stabilizing effect on yeast fermentation and a toughening effect on gluten. It is, incidentally, a required dough constituent under Food and Drug Administration standards, although salt-free bread is permitted for individuals on low-sodium diets. Almost all recipes in this book specify 1 or 2 teaspoons salt, but it is not an essential ingredient. Salt-free bread can be pretty dull stuff, however.

Fats

Lard, butter, oils, and margarine can generally be used interchangeably. Vegetable oils are convenient, but many bakers believe butter gives a better loaf texture. Fats and oils increase loaf volume, prevent crust cracking, enhance keeping qualities, and improve slicing qualities.

Sweeteners

When a recipe lists sugar, most bakers use granulated white sugar. But many other sweeteners can be substituted, including corn syrups and honey. Sugar is a yeast nutrient, although its primary function in baking is to influence flavor. Yeasts use the carbohydrates and starch in flour as their primary energy source, and too much sugar will actually inhibit, not stimulate, yeast fermentation.

Personalizing Breads

Today's bakers have a delicious selection of specialty baking ingredients available from around the country and around the world. Gourmet shops and health food stores stock exotic spices, unusual flours, nuts, berries, seeds, cheeses, and flavorings that make bread variations almost endless.

Dried cranberries, for example, are an excellent addition. It's odd how the oldest of things keeps popping up as something new. When the first Pilgrims arrived on the shores of North America, they found cranberries were being harvested by their new neighbors. The Native Americans used them with dried meat to make pemmican. Since the settlers thought the shape of the plant's blossoms looked like the head of a crane, they called the fruits "crane berries." Today they are used in all kinds of foods, including many bakery items, for their appearance, taste, and significant health benefits. Early medical practitioners prescribed them for the prevention of urinary tract infections, believing they acidified the urine and thus inhibited bacterial organisms. Modern medicine still endorses their effect on bacterial infections. In addition they are recognized as important sources of phytochemicals that reduce cellular damage and help prevent a number of degenerative diseases, including heart disease and cancer. In sourdoughs they produce some new and interesting flavors, especially when combined with other ingredients such as blueberries. You will find several suggestions in the recipe section.

One of the major advantages of doing your own baking is the ability to adjust the recipes to your own health standards. High-fiber grains such as oats may be added to many of the recipes. Steel-cut oats, for one example, produce a unique texture and distinctive flavor. To eliminate cholesterol, oil may be substituted for butter. You can also experiment with omitting eggs. Many people who once enjoyed baking bread have given it up because the temptation of hot bread was too hard on their diets. However, a slice of most home-baked sourdough breads contains no cholesterol and less than 150 calories. For a healthful, high-calorie, high-energy snack for kids, athletes, and back-packers, add nuts, seeds, raisins, dates, wheat germ, or anything else you want.

PUTTING IT ALL

Chapter 3

TOGETHER

As you balance success with frustration, remember my words in Chapter 2: The most important ingredient in baking real sourdoughs is the baker. There is more art (thank goodness) than science in baking as our ancestors did, and the artist learns by doing. But don't forget why you're here. Sourdoughs are for fun and personal satisfaction. Your first efforts may produce neither, but if you demand a real sourdough, it will come. Who are we home bakers? What differentiates us from commercial bakers and even from artisan bakers? The most obvious difference is economic. The artisans and the commercials must sell their breads at a profit. They must carefully monitor the quality of their ingredients against the expense. Quality will suffer if the costs are too high. Time does mean money in overhead and labor costs. The longer it takes the loaves to ferment, the less profit at the end of the day. San Francisco bakers used to rebuild their starters three times a day—every eight hours. It was not a requirement of the sourdough organisms, of course. More likely it was the length of one labor shift.

We home bakers have an enormous advantage. We pay ridiculous prices for just about everything: flour, baking dishes, special spices, how-to books (like this one), baking machines. We do it because we want the very best bread. We let our doughs ferment while we sleep until they are really ready, not half ready.

It is difficult to buy a sourdough bread that isn't flavored with vinegar or a variety of chemicals to simulate the real thing. You and I bake it in our kitchens with just wild sourdough cultures, recipes, flour, and water. What we bake is far better than almost anything we buy. But first we have to "put it altogether."

When I wrote *World Sourdoughs from Antiquity,* I emphasized activating dried cultures and culture preparation because they are critical in getting the organisms of the culture growing and reproducing. This is a chore almost unique to home bakers, since the challenge to artisan and commercial bakers is to *keep their cultures growing at a constant rate.* Remember, they bake daily or several times a day, usually seven days a week. If you and I bake once a week it's probably more frequent than the average home baker, and then the culture goes back to the refrigerator and become semidormant. The next time we use it, we have to get it back up to speed. In the last five years, I've learned several new tricks to do just that. Some of them are even done at room temperature. But you will probably still use a proofing box, and culture preparation is more important than ever.

Before You Start

Proofing Boxes

A proofing box is made from an inexpensive Styrofoam cooler. It will accurately regulate the temperature of proofing without the necessity of heating an entire room. Select a cooler large enough to fit upside down over your large mixing bowls (the lid is not used). I have several measuring 20½ by 13 inches and 11 inches deep. I use a General Electric twenty-five-watt flame-tip auradescent lightbulb connected to an ordinary dimmer switch. When I made my first proofing box, I simply cut a hole in the bottom of the cooler and pushed a light socket through it. In time, however, the heat of the socket eroded the hole, and now I have installed a standard porcelain lightbulb socket in all of my boxes.

This proofing box works extremely well, and although you will read a lot about room-temperature proofing in this book, the ability to warm a culture to 85° is invaluable. Whether you use a proofing box or leave your dough to rest at room temperature, be sure to have an accurate thermometer on hand (see page 37).

Culture Containers

Long-term storage of a mildly acid culture in a metal container may cause leaching of toxic ions and adversely affect the culture. Any glass, ceramic, or plastic container is acceptable if it is big enough and has a loose-fitting, but relatively secure, lid. Widemouthed quart canning jars are ideal because they are large enough to hold a bit more than three cups of culture, have a loose-fitting lid, and are relatively inexpensive. Furthermore I can get my hand inside one for cleaning. The lids should be replaced periodically if they become etched or if the rubber seals deteriorate. Don't tighten the lids of the containers. The cultures can build up pressure, particularly if the temperature rises, and crack the jars, although I have never had that happen.

Contrary to what you may have heard about sourdough prospectors, sourdough containers should be cleaned, if not regularly, at least occasionally. After many weeks of storage, containers build up a residue of dried culture and sometimes of mold. That's the time for a new jar and an occasion to clean the old one.

Ovens

Conventional ovens are usually gas or electric. I have a wood-burning Elmira Stove Works Oval as a backup for major power outages. No one disputes the advantage of steam-injected commercial ovens with humidity controls and all the bells and whistles. But most of us can't afford those luxuries and we manage to do pretty well without them. In *The Bread Builders, Hearth Loaves and Masonry Ovens,* Dan Wing and Allen Scott do an excellent job of extolling their masonry ovens, and I envy their skills.

Bowls and Utensils

Some myths are hard to shake, and the one about wooden spoons is at the top of the list. The acidity of sourdoughs will have absolutely no effect on metal spoons and bowls during the relatively short contact that occurs with mixing and kneading. After breaking the handles of my first half-dozen wooden spoons, I switched to metal and have never switched back. All of my bowls are plastic.

Baking Pans

Many of the recipes in this book are for 1½-pound loaves, which I bake in nonstick 8½ by 4½ by 2½-inch pans. Use this size pan, unless otherwise noted. These pans have a slight taper, making them a little smaller at the bottom. If you put the dough for a 1½-pound loaf in a pan intended for a 2-pound loaf, it obviously won't rise as high as you may be expecting. It is a small detail but worth keeping in mind. I also use what I call pup pans when I'm experimenting and don't want the larger loaves. The pups are also handy when you have a little extra dough. Mine measure 5¾ by 3 by 2 inches and are intended for about ½ pound of dough. Other standard pan sizes are large, 9 by 5 by 3 inches (2 pounds), and small, 7 by 3 by 2 inches (1½ pounds).

Baking Sheets

Also called cookie sheets, my sheets are nonstick and measure 17¼ by 11¼ by ¾ inches. I have at least a half dozen.

Thermometer

I have three thermometers, plus some backups. Two of them are inexpensive indoor-outdoor types that I use in proofing boxes and to record room temperature. I don't use the third one very much, but when I have needed it, I couldn't do without it. It's a digital thermometer with a 4½-inch probe that I have used to check the inner depths of a hot freshly baked loaf or a cold retarded dough. Baking is usually considered complete if the inner temperature is between 190° to 210°F. This one is a Taylor, Model 9840, with a range from negative 58° to 302° and a case and extra battery. I paid less than fifteen dollars at a local kitchen shop.

Cooling Racks

You need to put freshly baked loaves on wire cooling racks. Otherwise, they won't lose their moisture properly and will become soggy. Small round racks are inexpensive.

Baking Items You May Want

La Cloche

This is a stoneware baking dish, and it does almost as good a job as a masonry oven. So I bought one and was so impressed with the results that I agree, it's a must buy. La Cloche is the brand name found on two stoneware baking dishes, one that produces a round hearth loaf and the other an elongated French loaf. Both are covered dishes used in a conventional oven. They reproduce to some extent the characteristics of masonry ovens and do a beautiful job with sourdoughs. I have described my experiences with them in the recipe for La Cloche Sourdough (page 73).

Baking Stones

I have a 14 by 16-inch pizza stone that I use occasionally when I think I need a higher, more even temperature. This is particularly true for breads like pitas or free-form French loaves. Even then I tend to cheat a bit and proof my breads on a baking sheet and then put sheet and all on the stone.

Bread Machines

What's traditional about home bread machines? Take a peek at the January 1995 issue of *National Geographic*. There you will find the story of man's first leavened-bread bakery at the foot of the pyramids, and of our re-creation of that experience. We (and they) used huge clay bread molds that look just like the prototype of today's bread machines, and the clay molds were used in many an Egyptian's home five thousand years ago with a sourdough starter. It's hard to get more traditional than that. I evaluated several bread machines for this book, and you may be in for a surprise. If you use them correctly, they turn out some amazing sourdoughs. Chapter 5 includes comments on different machines and some secrets from those ancient pyramid builders.

Scales

I suspect a lot of us don't weigh most ingredients. I know I don't. But obviously we do measure just about everything and usually with measuring spoons and cups. But there are times when knowing the weight assumes some importance. The weight of some ingredients varies according to the environment, especially flours that tend to change significantly with humidity. A variety of relatively inexpensive kitchen scales accurate enough for baking are available. I inherited a postal scale that was displaced by a newer model, and I use it frequently when I'm feeling a little more picky.

Steps in Proofing

Activation and preparation—what's the difference? In previous books I described them separately, and some readers thought that once a few bubbles and a little foam appeared during activation, it was time to bake. It usually is not. Activation *starts* the process of getting a dried dormant culture back to normal activity, and culture preparation *completes* it and also is responsible for reactivating the cultures every time you take them from the refrigerator.

Activation

Let's start with a dried culture that you must activate by feeding with flour and water. You will only activate it once. This is a time to take a deep breath, lean back, and decide to take the necessary time to do it right. I use a 1-quart wide-mouthed canning jar. The dried culture is a mixture of concentrated organisms and the flour in which they were grown. It weighs 1 ounce and is approximately equivalent to ¼ cup of flour. I mix all of the dried culture with ¾ cup of flour and 1 cup of warm water (75° to 85°) thus yielding a 50/50 mixture of flour and water by volume. I stir this vigorously to whip air into the mixture and proof it in a warm place (about 85°) for 24 hours. I recommend activating at this temperature since the wet culture becomes acidified quickly, which limits contamination by other organisms that do not survive well in an acid medium. At the end of 24 hours, a few bubbles may appear on the surface as the first sign of growth and activity. In the next 24 hours growth will start to accelerate and the culture should be fed every 6 to 12 hours, again with vigorous stirring until there is a layer of foam and bubbles on top an inch or two thick. **Note: After the initial feeding the amount of flour changes to 1 cup and the water to ¾ cup to maintain the consistency.** The temperature is *critical* when activating, so read about proofing boxes (page 35). This may require several days and several feedings, depending primarily on the culture you are activating. This will be your "stock" culture. It will be the consistency of thick pancake batter, approximately 48 percent flour and 52 percent water, and is classified as a *liquid* culture. Put it in the refrigerator as soon as activation is complete to slow down the metabolism of the organisms and prevent them from using up the nutrients of the flour and returning to partial dormancy. It will be a reliable source of that culture as long as you take proper care of it. See page 8 for more information.

Now, if activating the culture by repeat feedings is continued until it becomes sufficiently active to start hitting the top of the jar (and only then), it may be used at once. If so, however, what you don't use in the recipe must be refrigerated immediately, as this is your stock culture.

Some cultures fully activate in 24 to 48 hours, while others may require 3 to 5 days. If the jar becomes two-thirds full, pour half of the culture into another jar, or you risk it running over the top. Then feed both halves until activated and keep one jar as a backup in case some accident destroys one of them. **Note: During long proofing either in a proofing box or at room temperature cultures tend to dry at the surface. This can be prevented by covering with a sheet of light plastic or dry towel. Do not use a damp towel or cloth since the evaporation will cool the culture.**

During the first step of activation the amount of flour added is almost four times the amount of dried culture, and contamination by organisms in the flour sometimes, although rarely, occurs. If this happens, it usually takes place in the first 24 hours and can produce sufficient bubbles and foam to suggest that the culture is activating. If there is a slightly unpleasant odor, and if the layer of "hooch" is at the bottom or in the middle of the fermenting culture, it indicates that contamination has probably occurred. Fortunately, it can usually be corrected by several "washings" and feedings.

Washing a Culture

Even with care, the culture is potentially contaminated by flour every time it is used. When a culture is refrigerated for long periods, and sometimes during the initial activation, these contaminants may overcome the sourdough organisms and form molds or produce unpleasant odors. Or if a culture is allowed to ferment at room temperature for a week or more, the metabolic products produced by the sourdough organisms may radically inhibit their further activity. These problems respond favorably to what I call "washing." After a thorough mixing, I dump everything except 1 cup of the culture from the jar. Next, I fill the jar with warm water while stirring vigorously. Then I again dump everything except 1 cup and feed the culture about 1 cup flour and ¾ cup water, stir it vigorously, and proof it at 85° for 6 to 12 hours. It may be necessary to repeat the process several times until the original culture becomes active.

Since many of my cultures have been relaxing in the refrigerator for 6 months, I always have to repeat this entire process for 3 to 6 days. When I'm doing this, I "grade" the activity of the culture from a trace, which means just a very few bubbles, to 4+, indicating full activity with a layer of foam and bubbles to the top of the jar. The reactivation process can be followed from the gradual increase in the foam layer until it literally booms to the top of the jar within 3 to 6 hours after the last wash. The old-timers called this "sweetening the pot," but I doubt if they did it exactly as I do today. The moral of this: When you take a month's vacation, you don't need a baby-sitter for your culture. But you may need these directions when you get back.

FEEDING STOCK CULTURES

When a culture is placed in the refrigerator, the yeast and lactobacilli become dormant. It is normal for a brownish liquid, the so-called hooch, to form on top of the culture. This mixture of organic alcohols forms during fermentation and has no adverse effect. Just mix it into the culture before using. After extended refrigeration, some of the organisms will be damaged and die. Therefore, it is desirable to have a high concentration at the start of cooling to produce a maximum number of cells that will regenerate when the culture is warmed. Whenever the stock culture is used, it should be fed before returning it to storage. I routinely feed it with 1 cup flour and ¾ cup water and proof it for 1 hour at room temperature before refrigeration.

Culture Preparation

LIQUID CULTURE

When it's time to bake, you don't repeat activation. Instead, you start with culture preparation. The stock culture in the refrigerator has a good concentration of cold yeast and lactobacilli, but it needs to be energized to a "working" culture, which has a higher level of growth and activity. This working culture performs almost equally well at either 85° in a proofing box or at room temperature of 68° to 72°. I take ½ cup of my cold liquid stock culture, put it in a bowl, and mix it with 1 cup flour and ½ cup water. This is the working culture. After I proof it for about 6 hours at 85°, or 12 hours at room temperature, I add another cup of flour plus ½ cup water. This time I proof it 4 hours at 85°, or 8 hours at room temperature. The culture is now "fully active" and teeming with sourdough organisms ready to make up the dough. Incidentally, the stock culture also gets some additional flour and water before it goes back into refrigeration (see page 41). Once activated and refrigerated, fast cultures, when warmed, may reach their peak activity in 2 to 4 hours, exhaust the flour nutrients, and become semidormant almost as fast. If you don't monitor the culture for 8 to 12 hours, you may miss this peak activity. The culture will appear flat, leading you to believe activation has not occurred. Usually tracks of foam left on the inside of the jar by the rising and falling layer of bubbles will point to the correct conclusion. A layer of hooch is normal and indicates the lactobacilli are active. Simply stir it back into the culture.

SPONGE CULTURE

As pointed out, the stock culture is refrigerated primarily to maintain its viability between periods of use. You can sustain it even longer by adding flour to the culture in the jar, making it much thicker just before cooling. Use only 1 jar of liquid culture for the sponge culture, and maintain a jar of liquid culture in case you need to wash it in the future to again make the sponge. I add 2 cups flour to 2 cups fully active liquid culture in a jar, mix it briefly, divide it between 2 jars, and refrigerate them immediately. This produces a very thick and sticky consistency that is approximately 65 percent flour and 35 percent water. I call it a sponge culture in contrast to the liquid culture described above. It will continue to ferment at refrigerator temperature for several hours, and it must be punched down occasionally to prevent it from running over the jar top.

If I use ½ cup of this culture, I obviously will be adding more flour to the dough than I do with ½ cup of a liquid culture. Therefore, I must reduce the amount of flour in the recipe accordingly.

Maintaining and Reactivating Stock Cultures

Whether one uses a liquid or a sponge culture is largely a matter of personal choice. The end result is much the same, although the sponge culture appears a little easier to reactivate after a month of storage. With its tacky consistency, it is also somewhat more difficult to handle. Instructions for using both cultures are found throughout the recipes section.

If my liquid culture has been refrigerated for more than 3 days when I am ready to use it, I maintain the *viability* by giving it a brief wash: The refrigerated jar is about half full. When I start to use it, I first fill the jar almost to the top with warm water while stirring vigorously. Then I split the contents of that jar between two other jars and add enough flour to each to restore the original consistency. Both jars then proof at room temperature for 1 hour. One goes back to the refrigerator and I use the other. If I don't use the one in the refrigerator for 2 to 4 weeks or longer, I may have to repeat several washes as described in Washing a Culture (page 40).

Sponge cultures maintain their viability in the refrigerator for at least 30 days. It may be necessary to remake this culture from an active liquid culture after 30 days or more or by reactivating it. My recipes made with a sponge culture start with ½ cup, which I reactivate by adding 1½ cups flour and 1 cup water followed by a 6- to 12-hour proof, depending on temperature. This is followed by another cup of flour with ¼ cup water and another proof of 4 to 8 hours. The culture is then ready to use or to go back to the refrigerator.

Commercial bakers use "retarding" (cooling) as a scheduling tool to help them hold their loaves overnight after a long day of toil. Early the next morning they warm them up and bake without having to go through the whole process again. Someone decided retarding actually improved the flavor and/or texture of the loaf, and currently it's the fashionable thing to do among some home bakers, too. I've tried it a number of times and have not been overly impressed. Occasionally it seems to have a favorable effect, and the next time I can't tell the difference between the retarded and the control loaf. Obviously there is a difference in proofing at 42°, but some activity of both yeast and lactobacilli does occur. Try retarding by putting your dough in the refrigerator overnight and see what you think.

The above examples will just get you started. There are a host of possibilities to produce a fully active starter. Not only can you choose different temperatures, but you can also experiment with different culture types, liquid or sponge, and decide on how much to use to produce the sourdoughs you prefer. Remember, longer fermentation produces more intense flavors, and smaller amounts of culture contribute to longer fermentations.

Steps in Baking

Consistency

Before we make bread dough, there is one other major consideration. In the above examples we dealt with activation, culture preparation, different temperatures, and proofing times. Of almost equal importance is the consistency of the dough and how you change and control it. If a dough is too soft and pliable, it will not hold its shape, especially with free-form loaves. If it is too stiff, it may resist the leavening gases and not rise as well as desired. The solution appears obvious: Add more flour or more water, depending on what appears to be needed. But how much? And, before you even begin mixing, is it possible to judge approximately how much flour and water will be needed to make a different number of loaves than the recipe specifies?

The best data I have seen on these questions appeared in a 1970 report, *"Nature of the San Francisco Sourdough French Bread Process,"* by Leo Kline and T. F. Sugihara. They described the recipe for "starter sponge" as consisting of 100 parts previous sponge, 100 parts flour, and 46 to 52 parts water by *weight,* which represents a ratio of 67 to 33, flour to water. In contrast the San Francisco dough has a ratio of 63 to 37, flour to water. The consistency of the starter doesn't make much difference, but the consistency of the dough determines many things about the finished loaf, so it is important to know how much flour is added with the starter. The reason for all this detail is to explain and promote the idea that a dough consistency of about 63 percent flour and 37 percent water is something worth achieving. Most of the recipes in this book are written to produce that consistency. In the appendix, I have included a sample template with instructions for converting any recipe for any amount of dough using any amount of starter to arrive at that same consistency. Now, for some more details you may need.

Kneading

Probably more has been written about kneading than any other aspect of bread making. And a lot of what has been written is wrong. First, why do we do it? There are two reasons: to incorporate sufficient flour into the dough to produce the right consistency and to develop the gluten. Both of those objectives are much easier to accomplish in the mixing bowl than on the well-floured board.

When I'm mixing a dough, the first thing I put in the bowl is the fully active culture. Then I add 2 or 3 cups of flour. I dissolve the salt in the warm water and pour that on top of the flour. I do it in that sequence specifically because I don't want to shock the culture with the osmotic pressure of a salty solution. Adding the flour between the culture and the salt solution creates a buffer zone of sorts when I start mixing. I stir that mixture vigorously—in fact I beat it until I feel it in my arms. After 4 to 5 minutes, the character of the mixture begins to change. The surface goes from shiny to a little dull and develops a slightly stippled appearance. Now when I add another cup of flour, the dough begins to thicken rapidly, and when I lift a mass of it with the mixing spoon, I can actually see the gluten matrix forming. In the recipes, this process is referred to as "mix and knead." At this point the dough is still sticky but getting a little too thick to manage with the spoon. I already have a cup of flour spread on my kneading board. I add my last cup to the bowl to reduce any stickiness, making the transfer to the board easier.

Most of the dough ends up in a mound of sorts, but a few globs and stray fragments always cling to the periphery. I tuck these into the mound, form an oval, and begin the process of kneading. As I work the dough back and forth it picks up flour from the board, and I push my hand into the mound to flatten it against the board and force in more flour. Then I fold over an edge, force that fold into the center, pick another spot, fold that over the previous fold, and round and round it goes. I've given up using the "satiny sheen" as a stopping point because I rarely see it anyway. Usually I make a serious attempt to incorporate as much flour as indicated in the recipe. But the push-pull routine I have just described is not very efficient in accomplishing that. Instead, I nail a portion of the dough to the board with one hand and rip open the surface of the mound by pushing with the heel of my other hand. This, of course, exposes the moist inner dough, which I flip over onto whatever flour remains. Then I turn it back over, fold the edges over the flour clinging to the exposed portion, and go back to my push-pull routine until it absorbs the excess. A few caveats: It is difficult to do it wrong, it is more difficult to do it too much, and it takes a little experience to get comfortable doing it. Most of us enjoy kneading. It is one of those mind-releasing exercises that contributes to the overall satisfaction of making bread.

You can overknead if you are using a power mixer. The dough will "slacken," and the resulting gluten will be of poor quality, letting a portion of the leavening gases escape. Power mixers and food processors vary markedly in their ability to handle sourdoughs, which are far more tenacious than bread doughs made with commercial yeast. Follow the instructions for your mixer carefully, but don't be surprised if sourdoughs overload it. I have even experienced significant problems with good heavy-duty equipment.

Forming Loaves

There are different ways to form dough into loaves, and most of them work. The objective is to produce a loaf—round, oval, oblong, or some other shape— with a skin that won't limit the expansion but will prevent the leavening gases from escaping as the loaf rises. To start, form the dough into a ball, which can be patted or pushed directly into the desired shape. I usually pat or roll the ball into a flat oval an inch or so thick and about as long as the pan I'm using. Then I simply fold it in half lengthwise and pinch the edges together. It goes into the pan seam side down, and from that point on the pan controls the shape.

I get quite a few questions from readers of our newsletter about problems with French loaves. Usually the baker asks, "How can I make my loaves rise up instead of sideways?" I've tried just about everything myself and it is not as easy as it might sound. Usually the consistency of the dough is too soft and it cannot support the weight of the rising dough so it expands sideways instead of vertically. The easy answer is to make the dough more firm by adding more flour. But there is a fine dividing line between too soft and too firm. If it is too firm or too dry, the upper surface limits expansion also. It obviously requires a bit of experimentation to get the consistency just right. I always lightly cover my loaves to keep that upper surface moist and pliable. I occasionally slash the surface as leavening starts to create an upward escape exit for the rising dough.

When all else fails, I will position three loaves side by side, put some type of block on the two outside loaves (a two-by-four is crude but effective) and the mass forces all three to rise vertically. On the other hand there are all kinds of gadgets and pans promoted to accomplish the same thing. Baguette pans, dough rising baskets, baker's couches, Italian bread pans and so on. Most of these work a little bit most of the time. I have several and most of them have been pushed to a back shelf. There is one exception and it really works splendidly, La Cloche. This is a heavy stoneware dish that turns out French type loaves like you won't believe. Go to page 38 for a complete description.

If the crust is too dry, the whole thing may lift slightly away from the body of the loaf as the dough rises. When the loaf bakes, cracks appear along the sides where the crust has separated. If you make a slash down the center of the loaf, the dough will rise through the slash instead of lifting the curst. This solves the problem and creates what most bakers consider an attractive appearance.

Slashing is an art in itself. You can make the slash as the loaf starts to leaven, which will produce a wider pattern as the dough rises. Or, you can do it just before baking, but this can cause a fragile loaf to retract partially unless done very carefully. It requires an extremely sharp edge, such as a single-edged razor blade or a surgical scalpel blade. Some kitchen-supply stores offer a lame, which is a handle with a disposable blade, for that specific purpose. But in my hands at least, lames have quickly lost their edge and not performed well. You can usually find disposable scalpel blades at reasonable prices from veterinary-supply stores and they work better.

Baking and Doneness

The recipe directions specify the time of baking and optimum temperature. Those times and temperatures are okay in my oven, in my kitchen at an elevation of about 5,000 feet, in the fairly dry environment of the Idaho mountains. But I did a lot of baking at sea level in highly humid Puget Sound areas without changing the recipes. Baking times and temperatures may still vary somewhat in your oven and environment and with your preference of doneness. So how do you determine when a loaf is ready to take out of the oven? You can use a digital thermometer with a probe. Temperatures between 190° to 210°F usually indicate that baking is complete. Sourdoughs made with just the culture, flour, and water brown very slightly. If the recipe contains a small amount of sugar or many other ingredients, the browning is better. So the answer to that question is trial and error in *your oven*. The directions in the recipes will always be close and small differences in time and temperature will make very little difference, but every time you make an error, or are successful, you will be a better baker the next time.

Crust Texture

The texture of the crust can be modified by different treatments before and during baking. Misting loaves with cool water from a spray bottle just before baking produces a firmer, chewy crust. I do this almost routinely at the start and twice more at 5-minute intervals. I spray the interior of the oven to increase the humidity at the same time. For a softer crust, brush the loaves lightly with melted butter or oil before putting them in the oven.

For a glossy, hard coating, mix 1 teaspoon cornstarch in ½ cup water. Heat the mixture to a boil, let cool, and brush it onto the loaves just before baking. A glaze made from a well-beaten egg produces a golden brown crust. For a deep brown, try brushing unbaked loaves with milk. Any of these glazes can be used just before baking and once or twice during baking. All of the crust modifications can be used as options regardless of whether the breads are pan loaves or free-form loaves. In addition I often do nothing at all, particularly if I want to taste the ingredients of the recipe in the crust a little better.

Care of a Heritage Sourdough

Your sourdough culture may be one, one hundred, or one thousand years old, and it cannot be easily destroyed except by too much heat. It should always be in the refrigerator, not on the kitchen counter, when not being used. Otherwise the organisms may completely utilize all of the available nutrients in the flour and become dormant or perish. Do not freeze your cultures, as some wild yeasts do not survive freezing and thawing.

Many home bakers use more than one sourdough culture and worry that one may contaminate and displace the organisms of the others. In general, I don't believe this is a significant problem. Stable cultures are characterized by organisms that have become dominant over extremely long periods of time with symbiotic relationships that are difficult to disrupt. Despite this, you should use some precautions to prevent gross contamination. Do not bake with different cultures at the same time. Avoid, with a passion, contaminating the culture with commercial yeasts or chemical leaveners. The symbiosis between wild yeast and lactobacilli can be destroyed by man-made yeast mutants or chemicals. Don't risk that possibility by adding such products to your cultures. Ironically, commercial bakers have just the opposite concern. They take extreme measures to prevent contamination of their cultures by wild yeast. Do not mix scraps or leftovers from bread dough into your cultures. The effect of salt, sugar, spices, and other ingredients on wild yeast is unpredictable and therefore undesirable.

RECIPES

Sourdough bakers are primarily concerned with flavor and texture. Flavor is directly related to the length of fermentation (proofing) and to the temperature of proofing. Texture is strongly affected by dough consistency, which is determined by the relative amounts of flour and water. From many experiments, I am becoming convinced that type of flour is also important. My comments (on page 13) emphasize that "weaker" all-purpose flours stretch more easily and create larger more irregular spaces in the dough. For this reason, in the ingredient lists of the following recipes, the terms white flour or just flour leaves the choice, all-purpose or bread flour, to the preference of the individual baker. The recipes that follow are designed to allow the baker a choice of proofing times and temperature. Longer fermentation produces a more intense flavor and lower temperatures may allow longer fermentation times. They have also been designed for optimum sourdough texture with a flour to water ratio of 63 percent flour to 37 percent water. The stock cultures are either liquid cultures, which are about 48 percent flour to 52 percent water, or sponge cultures, with 65 percent flour to 35 percent water.

It may surprise you to see many recipes starting with a very small amount of cold culture. Why do I do this? Remember one of the basic differences between home bakers and commercial bakers? The commercial guys, because they bake everyday, continuously propagate their leavens. After I use mine, I stick them in a refrigerator and after a week or so they are semidormant. But one essential step is not in the recipes. If my liquid culture has been in the refrigerator for more than 3 days, I always first give it a brief wash like this:

When I take it out, my quart jar will be ½ full. With vigorous stirring I add and mix warm water until the jar is about ¾ full. Then I transfer half of the contents to a second jar. To each jar I add 1 cup of flour and sufficient water to produce a moderately thick culture. Both jars will then be about ½ full. Both will proof at room temperature for about 1 hour. One will then go into the refrigerator for the next time. The other will be ready for immediate use. This brief wash ensures that the culture is not inhibited by too much acidity. If your culture has been unused for a month or more, you should expect to repeat the washing process several times. I handle the sponge cultures a little differently. They are very thick and age a little better than liquid cultures. If I have used a sponge culture within a month, I rely on the first two steps in the recipe instructions to perform the culture preparation. Of course, that means I don't automatically duplicate another sponge for the next time I want one. Instead, periodically, I get a liquid culture up to full steam and put it to bed with an excess of flour thus creating my next sponge. Almost all of the recipes start with a cold culture, whether liquid or sponge. Why cold? Simple. If it has been 3 days or more since you last used that culture, it should be in the refrigerator and cold. When you start to bake, each recipe takes you through the essential steps of culture preparation that ensure an active culture as you add the final ingredients to the dough.

Previously I warmed the cultures up and reactivated them by feeding as much as 2 cups of warm culture for various periods of time until it looked active, and I usually ended up with more or less than I actually needed in the recipe. Now when I start out with ½ cup of cold culture, I'm really going into a culture preparation step that will produce exactly the amount of culture needed for the final recipe (see culture preparation, page 41). That doesn't mean I always do it that way, and neither should you. If a liquid culture has been in storage for a long time, it usually needs washing (page 40), perhaps several times, to rid it of excess acidity. By the time it gets back to a fully active stage, it is ready to use, and my recipe will start with 2 cups of that warm culture.

If you use a different amount of culture or desire to make a different amount of dough, the amounts of flour and water must be changed to maintain the correct consistency. A consistency template is an easy way to adjust the flour and water to maintain the ratio of 63 percent flour to 37 percent water. The template and instructions for its use are in the Appendix. Never rely implicitly on one of my recipes. My flours may be a little drier or my cultures a little thicker or thinner than yours on any given day. Trust your instincts. If a dough looks a little too thin or thick, add more flour or more water. You will learn every time you are right (or wrong) and next time you will profit from the experience. You are the baker!

These recipes by no means exhaust the possibilities. With some cultures, after 12 hours of proofing, you could mix and knead in another cup of flour plus ½ cup of water and proof it for another 12 hours. For those who cherish sourness, this is a good option. Like every other baker, I have favorite recipes and tips on how to make them better. Here is a list of my top ten in no particular order.

1. World Bread (page 54)
2. Light Swedish Limpa (page 76)
3. Tanya's Peasant Black Bread (page 90)
4. English Muffin (page 124)
5. Dinner Rolls (page 129)
6. Cranberry-Huckleberry Batter Bread (page 148)
7. Yukon Flapjacks (page 157)
8. Sour Cream Waffles (page 164)
9. Khubz Arabi (Arab Bread) (page 134)
10. San Francisco Sourdough in a bread machine (page 177) and by hand (page 56)

GENERAL RECIPES

WORLD BREAD

RECIPE WITH **SPONGE** CULTURE   Makes two 1½-pound loaves

This recipe is an introduction to wild sourdoughs for novice and experienced baker alike. Once mastered, you will be ready to experiment with any recipe that follows. World Bread will convince any skeptic that all sourdough cultures are not the same. It is a basic white bread recipe used throughout the world. The culture you choose (and the method) will give the bread its flavor and texture. If you are interested in using the recipe to compare different cultures, try to eliminate all other variables. Then set up a taste panel of your friends as judges. Code the loaves so the testers are not influenced by the source or name of the culture.

Two quite different proofing temperatures with different schedules are suggested. There are many others you can try. Keep in mind that the milk in the recipe should not be used in a long proofing cycle. It is added here when the final recipe is made and the loaves are formed. The recipe calls simply for white flour. Use your preference, bread or all-purpose flour.

½ cup cold sponge culture	1 cup milk
1¼ cups water	2 teaspoons salt
6 cups white flour	2 tablespoons sugar
2 tablespoons butter or vegetable oil	

1. Mix the sponge culture with 1½ cups of the flour and 1 cup of the water in a large mixing bowl. This is the working culture. Proof 12 hours at room temperature (68° to 72°) or 6 hours in a proofing box at 85°.

2. Add 1 cup flour and the remaining ¼ cup water. Mix and knead until smooth. Proof 12 hours at room temperature or 6 hours in the proofing box. After proofing, this is the fully active culture.

3. Punch down. Chop the butter into small pieces and add to the milk. Warm briefly to 75° to 85° until the butter melts. Add the salt and sugar and stir until dissolved. Mix this mixture into the dough. Reserve 1 cup of the flour for flouring the board. Mix and spoon knead the remaining

flour into the dough 1 cup at a time. When too stiff to mix by hand, transfer to the floured board and knead in the remaining flour.

4.   Form 2 pan loaves, and proof at the same temperature used above until the dough rises above the pan tops (2½ to 4 hours).

5.   Bake in a preheated oven at 375° for 40 to 45 minutes. Remove from the pans and cool on wire racks.

SAN FRANCISCO SOURDOUGH BREAD

RECIPE WITH **LIQUID** CULTURE   Makes two 1½-pound loaves

The American Institute of Baking describes San Francisco sourdough as the benchmark by which all other sourdough breads are judged, and I am in full agreement. Largely because of that, I have included two slightly different recipes, one by hand and one by machine. The reputation of this sourdough is, indeed, worldwide. To achieve the fabulous flavor, it requires the organisms of that culture. We call ours the Original San Francisco culture.

½ cup cold liquid culture	2 cups water
6 cups flour	1½ teaspoons salt

1. Mix the liquid culture with 1 cup of the flour and ½ cup of the water in a large mixing bowl. This is the working culture. Proof 12 hours at room temperature (68° to 72°) or 6 hours in a proofing box at 85°.

2. Add 1 cup of the flour and ½ cup of the water. Mix and knead until smooth. Proof 8 hours at room temperature or 4 hours in the proofing box. After proofing, this is the fully active culture.

3. Punch down. Dissolve the salt in the remaining 1 cup water and mix into the dough. Reserve 1 cup of the flour for flouring the board. Mix and spoon knead the remaining 3 cups flour into the dough 1 cup at a time. When too stiff to mix by hand, transfer to the floured board and knead in the remaining flour.

4. Form 2 pan loaves or French loaves, and proof them at the same temperature used above until ready to bake (3 to 4 hours).

5. Bake in a preheated oven at 375° for 40 to 45 minutes. Remove from the pans and cool on wire racks.

≈   *Note:* If you really want sour sourdough, repeat step 2, adding another 1 cup of flour and ½ cup of water.

AUSTRIAN WHEAT-RYE BREAD

RECIPE WITH **LIQUID** CULTURE   Makes two 1½-pound loaves

The combination of white and rye flours produces a moderate rye flavor. The bread rises well but results in a somewhat heavier loaf than an all-wheat bread. The addition of anise and caraway imparts the typical flavor characteristic of a European rye loaf.

2 cups rye flour	*1½ teaspoons salt*
2¾ cups white flour	*2 tablespoons sugar*
2 cups cold liquid culture	*1 tablespoon caraway seeds*
½ cup water	*1 teaspoon aniseeds*
¾ cup milk	*1 teaspoon ground cumin*

1. Combine the flours and mix well. Mix the liquid culture with 1 cup of the flour mixture and ¼ cup of the water in a large mixing bowl. This is the working culture. Proof 12 hours at room temperature (68° to 72°) or 6 hours in a proofing box at 85°.

2. Add 1 cup of the flour mixture and ¼ cup of the water. Mix and knead until smooth. Proof 8 hours at room temperature or 4 hours in the proofing box. After proofing, this is the fully active culture.

3. Punch down. Mix together the milk, salt, sugar, caraway seeds, aniseeds, and cumin. Add to the dough and mix well. Reserve 1 cup of the flour mixture for flouring the board. Mix and spoon knead the remaining 1¾ cups flour mixture into the dough 1 cup at a time. When too stiff to mix by hand, transfer to the floured board and knead in the remaining flour mixture.

4. Form 2 pan loaves, and proof them at the same temperature used above until the dough rises about 1 inch above the pan tops (2½ to 3 hours).

5. Bake in a preheated oven at 375° for 40 to 45 minutes. Remove from the pans and cool on wire racks.

CARAWAY RYE BREAD

RECIPE WITH **LIQUID** CULTURE   Makes two 1½-pound loaves

Few ingredients make a better combination than caraway and rye. Although many of these recipes utilize caraway, this one particularly enhances the two flavors.

2 cups light rye flour	*1½ teaspoons salt*
2¾ cups white flour	*¾ cup dark molasses*
2 cups cold liquid culture	*2 tablespoons butter, melted*
1¼ cups water	*2 tablespoons caraway seeds*

1. Combine the flours and mix well. Mix the liquid culture with 1 cup of the flour mixture and ¼ cup of the water in a large mixing bowl. This is the working culture. Proof 12 hours at room temperature (68° to 72°) or 6 hours in a proofing box at 85°.

2. Add 1 cup of the flour mixture and ½ cup of the water. Mix and knead until smooth. Proof 8 hours at room temperature or 4 hours in the proofing box. After proofing, this is the fully active culture.

3. Punch down. Mix ½ cup water, the salt, molasses, butter, and caraway seeds. Add to the dough and mix well. Reserve 1 cup of the flour mixture for flouring the board. Mix and spoon knead the remaining 1¾ cups flour mixture into the dough 1 cup at a time. When too stiff to mix by hand, transfer to the floured board and knead in the remaining flour mixture.

4. Form 2 pan loaves, and proof them at the same temperature used above until the dough rises about 1 inch above the pan tops (2½ to 3 hours).

5. Bake in a preheated oven at 400° for 45 to 50 minutes. Remove from the pans and cool on wire racks.

CHEESE BREAD

RECIPE WITH **LIQUID** CULTURE   Makes one 2-pound loaf

Cheese breads are a pleasant variation. This one is lightly leavened.

2 cups cold liquid culture   *1 teaspoon salt*
½ cup water   *3 cups white flour*
2 tablespoons oil   *8 ounces cream cheese, softened*
2 teaspoons sugar

Glaze

1 egg, beaten
Sesame seeds

1. Mix the liquid culture with the water, oil, sugar, and salt in a large mix-ing bowl.

2. Reserve 1 cup of the flour for flouring the board. Add flour to the culture mixture 1 cup at a time and mix and spoon knead until too stiff to mix by hand. Transfer to the floured board and knead in the remaining flour.

3. Shape into a round, place it in a large bowl, cover lightly with plastic wrap and proof 12 hours at room temperature (68° to 72°) or 6 hours in a proofing box at 85°.

4. Punch down. Flatten by hand and with a rolling pin into a rectangle ½ thick.

5. Spread the cheese over the dough rectangle, leaving a 1-inch border uncovered on all sides. Roll up from the long side and pinch the ends to seal, forming an oval, elongate loaf.

6. Place on a baking sheet and proof 4 hours at room temperature or 1½ hours in the proofing box.

7. To glaze the loaf, brush the top with beaten egg and sprinkle with sesame seeds.

8. Bake in preheated oven at 375° for 40 to 45 minutes. Cool on a wire rack.

CHEESE-ONION BREAD

RECIPE WITH **LIQUID** CULTURE   Makes two 1½-pound loaves

Adding freshly chopped green onion to a cheese bread yields a truly delicious loaf. The onion adds liquid, which sometimes requires the addition of more flour. Test a loaf with a digital thermometer when it is removed from the oven. The center should be 190°. Toast the slices for a right-out-of-the-oven aroma. This dough can also be braided.

2 cups cold liquid culture
4¾ cups white flour
½ cup water
¾ cup milk
2 tablespoons sugar

1 teaspoon salt
2 tablespoons butter, melted
2 cups loosely packed Cheddar cheese
1 cup finely chopped green onion

1. Mix the liquid culture with 1 cup of flour and ¼ cup of the water in a large mixing bowl. This is the working culture. Proof 12 hours at room temperature (68° to 72°) or 6 hours in a proofing box at 85°.

2. Add 1 cup of the flour and the remaining ¼ cup water. Mix and knead until smooth. Proof 8 hours at room temperature or 4 hours in the proofing box. After proofing, this is the fully active culture.

3. Punch down. Mix together the milk, sugar, salt, butter, Cheddar cheese, and onion. Add to the dough and mix well. Reserve 1 cup of the flour for flouring the board. Mix and spoon knead the remaining 1¾ cups flour into the dough 1 cup at a time. When too stiff to mix by hand, transfer to the floured board and knead in the remaining flour.

4. Form 2 pan loaves, and proof them at the same temperature used above until the dough rises about 1 inch above the pan tops (2½ to 3 hours).

5. Bake in a preheated oven at 375° for 40 to 45 minutes. Remove from the pans and cool on wire racks.

CINNAMON-RAISIN NUT BREAD

RECIPE WITH **LIQUID** CULTURE   Makes two 1½-pound loaves

This is an excellent bread for morning toast.

2 cups cold liquid culture   *1½ teaspoons salt*
4¾ cups white flour   *2 tablespoons sugar*
½ cup water   *¼ cup ground cinnamon*
2 tablespoons butter, melted   *1 cup chopped nuts*
¾ cup milk   *1 cup raisins*

Filling
2 tablespoons ground
   cinnamon
½ cup sugar

1. Mix the liquid culture with 1 cup of the flour and ¼ cup of the water in a large mixing bowl. This is the working culture. Proof 12 hours at room temperature (68° to 72°) or 6 hours in a proofing box at 85°.

2. Add 1 cup of the flour and the remaining ¼ cup water. Mix and knead until smooth. Proof 8 hours at room temperature or 4 hours in the proofing box. After proofing, this is the fully active culture.

3. Punch down. Mix together the milk, salt, 2 tablespoons sugar, ¼ cup cinnamon, nuts, and raisins. Add to the dough and mix well. Reserve 1 cup of the flour for flouring the board. Mix and spoon knead 1 cup of flour at a time. When too stiff to mix by hand, transfer to the floured board and knead in the remaining flour.

4. Divide the dough in half. Roll out each half into a rectangle the width of a loaf pan (8½ by 4½ by 2½-inch pan) and about ½ inch thick.

5. To make the filling, mix the 2 tablespoons cinnamon with ½ cup sugar. Sprinkle half of this mixture on each rectangle and roll up to form loaves.

6. Place the loaves in the pans, and proof at the same temperature used above until the dough rises about 1 inch above the pan tops (2½ to 3 hours).

7. Bake in a preheated oven at 375° for 50 to 55 minutes. Remove from the pans and cool on wire racks.

CRANBERRY-NUT SOURDOUGH

RECIPE WITH **LIQUID** CULTURE   Makes two 1½ pound-loaves

The choice of nuts is yours. I've tried this bread with both almonds and walnuts separately. The mix with cranberries is a good one.

2 cups cold liquid culture
4¾ cups flour
1¼ cups water
1½ teaspoons salt

2 tablespoons sugar
½ cup sweetened dried
*   cranberries*
½ cup chopped nuts

1. Mix the liquid culture with 1 cup of the flour and ¼ cup of the water in a large mixing bowl. This is the working culture. Proof 12 hours at room temperature (68° to 72°) or 6 hours in a proofing box at 85°.

2. Add 1 cup of the flour and ½ cup of the water. Proof 8 hours at room temperature or 4 hours in the proofing box. After proofing, this is the fully active culture.

3. Punch down. Mix together the remaining ½ cup water, the salt, sugar, cranberries, and nuts. Add to the dough and mix well. Reserve 1 cup of the flour for flouring the board. Mix and spoon knead the remaining 1¾ cups flour into the dough 1 cup at a time. When too stiff to mix by hand, transfer to the floured board and knead in the remaining flour.

4. Form 2 pan loaves, and proof at the same temperature used above until the dough rises about 1 inch above the pan tops (2½ to 3 hours).

5. Bake in a preheated oven at 375° for 40 to 45 minutes. Remove from the pans and cool on wire racks.

CRANBERRY-BLUEBERRY RYE

RECIPE WITH **LIQUID** CULTURE   Makes two 1½-pound loaves

Frozen blueberries or huckleberries are preferred over canned ones, although fresh ones, if you are so fortunate, will do just fine. These berries, along with a light touch of rye, make a fabulous sourdough.

2 cups light rye flour
2¾ cups flour
2 cups cold liquid culture
1¼ cups water

1½ teaspoons salt
½ cup sweetened dried cranberries
½ cup frozen blueberries or
*   huckleberries*

1. Combine the flours and mix well. To make the working culture, mix the liquid culture with 1 cup of the flour mixture and ¼ cup of the water in a large mixing bowl. Proof 12 hours at room temperature (68° to 72°) or 6 hours in a proofing box at 85°.

2. Add 1 cup of the flour mixture and ½ cup of the water. Mix and knead until smooth. Proof 8 hours at room temperature or 4 hours in the proofing box. After proofing, this is the fully active culture.

3. Punch down. Dissolve the salt in the remaining ½ cup water and mix with all the berries. Add to the dough and mix well. Reserve 1 cup of the flour mixture for flouring the board. Mix and spoon knead the remaining 1¾ cups flour mixture into the dough 1 cup at a time. When too stiff to mix by hand, transfer to the floured board and knead in the remaining flour.

4. Form 2 pan loaves, and proof them at the same temperature used above until the dough rises about 1 inch above the pan tops (2½ to 3 hours).

5. Bake in a preheated oven at 375° for 40 to 45 minutes. Remove from the pan and cool on wire racks.

DATE BREAD

RECIPE WITH **LIQUID** CULTURE   Makes one 2-pound loaf

Dates are the fruit of the desert. This recipe has them in a loaf leavened by wild yeast, which, in the case of my loaf, uses Sourdoughs International's from Saudi Arabia. This is a heavy dough and shouldn't be hurried.

½ cup cold liquid culture	*1 cup chopped nuts*
1¼ cups water	*¼ cup sugar*
2 tablespoons oil	*1 teaspoon salt*
1 cup chopped dates	*3¾ cups white flour*

1. Mix the liquid culture with the water, oil, dates, nuts, sugar, and salt in a large mixing bowl.

2. Reserve 1 cup of the flour for flouring the board. Add the remaining 2¾ cups flour to the culture mixture 1 cup at a time and mix and spoon knead until too stiff to mix by hand. Transfer to the floured board and knead in the remaining flour.

3. Shape into a round and proof 12 hours at room temperature (68° to 72°) or 6 hours in a proofing box at 85°.

4. Punch down. Form a pan loaf (use a 9 by 5 by 3-inch pan in this recipe), and proof at the same temperature used above until the dough rises about 1 inch above the pan top (3 to 4 hours).

5. Bake in a preheated oven at 375° for 55 to 60 minutes, remove from the pan, and cool on a wire rack.

FRENCH BREAD I

RECIPE WITH **LIQUID** CULTURE   Makes two 1¹/₂-pound loaves

Sourdough breads fell out of favor in French cities after the turn of the twentieth century when commercial yeast became available. Sourdoughs are now back in vogue, however, and, once again, prevail in the country's smaller bakeries. Much has been written about the difficulties of emulating the French bakery, with its steam ovens and special brick. Fear not! You can produce an authentic French loaf in your own culture with your own steam. This really works. Here I use our culture from France with two slightly different recipes.

> 2 cups cold liquid culture   1¼ cups water
> 4¾ cups flour   1 teaspoon salt

1. Mix the liquid culture with 1 cup of the flour and ¼ cup of the water in a large mixing bowl. This is the working culture. Proof 12 hours at room temperature (68° to 72°) or 6 hours in a proofing box at 85°.

2. Add 1 cup of the flour and ¼ cup of the water. Proof 8 hours at room temperature or 4 hours in the proofing box. After proofing, this is the fully active culture.

3. Punch down. Dissolve the salt in the remaining ¾ cup water. Add to the dough and mix well. Reserve 1 cup of the flour for flouring the board. Mix and spoon knead the remaining 1¾ cups flour into the dough 1 cup at a time. When too stiff to mix by hand, transfer to the floured board and knead in the remaining flour.

4. Form 2 pan loaves or French loaves, and proof at the same temperature used above until the dough rises about 1 inch above the pan tops (2½ to 3 hours).

5. Bake in a preheated oven at 375° for 40 to 45 minutes; spritz the loaves and the oven at start of baking and twice more at 5-minute intervals. Remove from the pans and cool on wire racks.

FRENCH BREAD II

RECIPE WITH **SPONGE** CULTURE   Makes two 1¹/₂-pound loaves

½ cup cold sponge culture   *2¼ cups water*
6 cups white flour   *1 teaspoon salt*

1. Mix the sponge culture with 1½ cups of the flour and 1 cup of the water. This is the working culture. Proof 12 hours at room temperature (68° to 72°) or 6 hours in a proofing box at 85°.

2. Add 1 cup of the flour and ¼ cup of the water. Mix well and proof 8 hours at room temperature or 4 hours in the proofing box. After proofing, this is the fully active culture.

3. Punch down. Dissolve the salt in the remaining 1 cup water. Add to the dough and mix well. Reserve 1 cup of the flour for flouring the board. Mix and spoon knead the remaining 2½ cups flour into the dough 1 cup at a time. When too stiff to mix by hand, transfer to the floured board and knead in the remaining flour.

4. Form loaves, proof, bake, and cool as directed for Recipe I.

FINNISH RYE BREAD

RECIPE WITH **SPONGE** CULTURE   Makes two 1½-pound loaves

The addition of brown sugar imparts a golden brown color and enhances the flavor of this moderately heavy rye bread. It may rise slowly. It is a favorite in Scandinavia, where long winters allow plenty of time for proofing. Naturally, I make this with our Finnish culture.

3 cups rye flour
3 cups white flour
½ cup cold sponge culture
1¼ cups water
1 cup milk

1½ teaspoons salt
¾ cup firmly packed brown
*   sugar*
2 tablespoons butter, melted

1. Combine the flours and mix well. To make the working culture, mix the sponge culture with 1½ cups of the flour mixture and 1 cup of the water in a large mixing bowl. Proof 12 hours at room temperature (68° to 72°) or 6 hours in a proofing box at 85°.

2. Add 1 cup of the flour mixture and ¼ cup of the water. Mix and knead until smooth. Proof 12 hours at room temperature or 6 hours in the proofing box. After proofing, this is the fully active culture.

3. Punch down. Mix together the milk, salt, brown sugar, and butter. Add to the dough and mix well. Reserve 1 cup of the flour mixture for flouring the board. Mix and spoon knead the remaining 2½ cups flour into the dough 1 cup at a time. When too stiff to mix by hand, transfer to the floured board and knead in the remaining flour.

4. Form 2 pan loaves or French loaves, and proof them at the same temperature used above until ready to bake (2½ to 4 hours).

5. Bake in a preheated oven at 375° for 40 to 45 minutes. Remove from the pans and cool on wire racks.

GERMAN CHRISTMAS BREAD

RECIPE WITH **LIQUID** CULTURE   Makes one 3-pound loaf

Sweet yeast breads from Germany are known as stollens throughout Europe. A sourdough sweet Christmas bread may strike you as an oxymoron. Maybe it is, but try it and be surprised. You can substitute a mixture of candied fruits for the citron. Top with a glaze of your choice.

2 cups cold liquid culture   *½ cup currants*
4¾ cups white flour   *½ cup candied citron*
½ cup water   *Grated zest of 1 lemon*
¾ cup milk   *½ teaspoon ground cinnamon*
½ cup butter, melted   *½ teaspoon ground cloves*
2 teaspoons salt   *½ teaspoon ground cardamom*
½ cup raisins

1. Mix the liquid culture with 1 cup of the flour and ¼ cup of the water in a large mixing bowl. This is the working culture. Proof 12 hours at room temperature (68° to 72°) or 6 hours in a proofing box at 85°.

2. Add 1 cup of the flour and the remaining ¼ cup water. Proof 8 hours at room temperature or 4 hours in the proofing box. After proofing, this is the fully active culture.

3. Punch down. Mix together the milk, butter, salt, raisins, currants, citron, lemon zest, and ground spices. Add to the dough and mix well. Reserve 1 cup of the flour for flouring the board. Mix and spoon knead the remaining 1¾ cups flour into the dough 1 cup at a time. When too stiff to mix by hand, transfer to the floured board and knead in the remaining flour.

4. Form an oblong loaf, place on a baking sheet, and proof at the same temperature used above until the dough is doubled in volume (3 to 4 hours).

5. Bake in a preheated oven at 375° for 50 to 55 minutes. Cool on a wire rack.

6. You may top the loaf with a glaze of your choice while it is still warm.

GERMAN RYE BREAD

RECIPE WITH **SPONGE** CULTURE   Makes two 1½-pound loaves

For those who prefer a more subtle and delicate rye flavor, a single cup of rye flour is ideal. This bread rises well and is a favorite in southern Austria and Germany. I use our culture from Austria in this one.

1 cup rye flour	1 cup milk
5 cups white flour	2 teaspoons salt
½ cup cold sponge culture	2 tablespoons vegetable oil
1¼ cups water	2 tablespoons molasses

1. Combine the flours and mix well. To make the working culture, mix the sponge culture with 1½ cups of the flour mixture and 1 cup of the water in a large mixing bowl. Proof 12 hours at room temperature (68° to 72°) or 6 hours in a proofing box at 85°.

2. Add 1 cup of the flour mixture and the remaining ¼ cup water. Mix and knead until smooth. Proof 12 hours at room temperature or 6 hours in the proofing box. After proofing, this is the fully active culture.

3. Punch down. Mix together the milk, salt, oil, and molasses. Add to the dough and mix well. Reserve 1 cup of the flour mixture for flouring the board. Mix and spoon knead the remaining 2½ cups flour mixture into the dough 1 cup at a time. When too stiff to mix by hand, transfer to the floured board and knead in the remaining flour.

4. Form 2 pan loaves or French loaves, and proof them at the same temperature used above until ready to bake (2½ to 4 hours).

5. Bake in a preheated oven at 375° for 40 to 45 minutes. Remove from the pans and cool on wire racks.

GRAHAM AND CRACKED-WHEAT BREAD

RECIPE WITH **LIQUID** CULTURE   Makes two 1½-pound loaves

Cracked wheat is produced by a cutting process, rather than grinding. It can be used raw, as in this recipe, or cooked. If cooked, it is usually presoaked for several hours and then simmered for about 1 hour in 2 cups water for every cup of cracked grain.

1 cup graham flour	*2 tablespoons sugar*
3¾ cups white flour	*½ cup dark molasses*
2 cups cold liquid culture	*2 tablespoons butter, melted*
½ cup water	*¼ cup cracked wheat, uncooked*
¾ cup milk	*or cooked*
1½ teaspoons salt	

1. Combine the flours and mix well. To make the working culture, mix the liquid culture with 1 cup of flour mixture and ¼ cup of the water in a large mixing bowl. Proof 12 hours at room temperature (68° to 72°) or 6 hours in a proofing box at 85°.

2. Add 1 cup of the flour mixture and the remaining ¼ cup water. Mix and knead until smooth. Proof 8 hours at room temperature or 4 hours in the proofing box. After proofing, this is the fully active culture.

3. Punch down. Mix together the milk, salt, sugar, molasses, butter, and cracked wheat. Add to the dough and mix well. Reserve 1 cup of the flour mixture for flouring the board. Mix and spoon knead the remaining 1¾ cups flour mixture into the dough 1 cup at a time. When too stiff to mix by hand, transfer to the floured board and knead in the remaining flour.

4. Form into 2 pan loaves, and proof at the same temperature used above until the dough rises about 1 inch above the pan tops (2½ to 3 hours).

5. Bake in a preheated oven at 375° for 40 to 45 minutes. Remove from the pans and cool on wire racks.

HERB BREAD

RECIPE WITH **LIQUID** CULTURE   Makes two 1½-pound loaves

This delightful loaf uses an aromatic mixture of thyme, oregano, and basil.

2 cups cold liquid culture	*1 teaspoon salt*
4¾ cups white flour	*2 teaspoons sugar*
½ cup water	*1 teaspoon dried thyme*
¾ cup milk	*1 teaspoon dried oregano*
2 tablespoons butter, melted	*1 teaspoon dried basil*

1. Mix the liquid culture with 1 cup of the flour and ¼ cup of water in a large mixing bowl. This is the working culture. Proof 12 hours at room temperature (68° to 72°) or 6 hours in a proofing box at 85°.

2. Add 1 cup of the flour and the remaining ¼ cup water. Mix and knead until smooth. Proof 8 hours at room temperature or 4 hours in the proofing box. After proofing, this is the fully active culture.

3. Punch down. Mix together the milk, butter, salt, sugar, and dried herbs. Add to the dough and mix well. Reserve 1 cup of the flour for flouring the board. Mix and spoon knead the remaining 1¾ cups flour into the dough 1 cup at a time. When too stiff to mix by hand, transfer to the floured board and knead in the remaining flour.

4. Form 2 pan loaves, and proof at the same temperature used above until the dough rises about 1 inch above the pan tops (2½ to 3 hours).

5. Bake in a preheated oven at 375° for 40 to 45 minutes. Remove from the pans and cool on wire racks.

LA CLOCHE SOURDOUGH

RECIPE WITH **SPONGE** CULTURE   Makes 1 fabulous French loaf

In *The Bread Builders, Hearth Loaves and Masonry Ovens,* Daniel Wing has nothing but praise for La Cloche. Because Wing is a leading advocate of masonry ovens, his endorsement is worth investigating. La Cloche is somewhat analogous to the home bread machine, in that, like the bread machine, you can only bake one loaf at a time. It is a heavy stoneware baking dish made in two styles, one oval for hearth breads and the other oblong (14½ by 5¼ by 7 inches) for French- or Italian-type loaves. Both styles are equipped with lids. They are a little pricey but they do a terrific job.

> *½ cup cold sponge culture*   *2½ cups water*
> *6½ cups white flour*   *2 teaspoons salt*

1. Mix the sponge culture with 1½ cups of the flour and 1 cup of the water in a large mixing bowl. This is the working culture. Proof 12 hours at room temperature (68° to 72°) or 6 hours in a proofing box at 85°.

2. Add 1 cup of the flour and ½ cup of the water. Mix and knead until smooth. Shape into a round, place it in a large bowl, cover lightly with plastic wrap, and proof 12 hours at room temperature or 6 hours in the proofing box. After proofing, this is the fully active culture.

3. Punch down. Dissolve the salt in the remaining 1 cup water. Add to the dough and mix well. Reserve 1 cup of the flour for flouring the board. Mix and spoon knead the remaining 3 cups flour into the dough 1 cup at a time. When too stiff to mix by hand, transfer to the floured board and knead in the remaining flour.

4. Form a French loaf about 14 inches long, carefully place it in the covered La Cloche, and proof at the same temperature used above until ready to bake (2½ to 4 hours). I proofed it at room temperature and sneaked an occasional peek under the lid to see how it was doing.

5. Bake in a preheated oven at 500° with the lid in place. After 30 minutes,

reduce the heat to about 400°, remove the lid, and continue baking for 15 minutes, or until the crust is browned. Remove the loaf from the bakery dish and cool on a wire rack.

≈ *Note:* Some bakers preheat both pieces, the dish and the lid, to 425° and flip the dough into La Cloche from a proofing basket. That sounds like it would take a little practice. Proofing it in La Cloche was very easy, of course, and the results were, as guaranteed, fabulous. It is worth the effort and cost. But I have a confession: The recipe as given above produces about 3 pounds, 6 ounces of dough. After several attempts I am forced to admit La Cloche will not restrain more than 2 pounds 6 ounces of dough and the final loaf will weigh 2 pounds, 2½ ounces. So why didn't I change the recipe? That extra pound of dough makes a great little loaf that I can sample right out of the oven and save my masterpiece until the company arrives. Now if you can't live with that, simply reduce the recipe to 4¼ cups flour and 1½ cups of water and you will end up with just the right amount for La Cloche.

MALT BEER BREAD

RECIPE WITH **LIQUID** CULTURE   Makes two 1¹/₂-pound loaves

Experiment with different beers for making this bread. I've used dark beers from Germany and Scandinavia to complement the rye flavor, but many of the local beers now produced by American microbreweries are as good.

2¾ cups white flour
2 cups rye flour
2 cups cold liquid culture
1¼ cups malt beer

1½ teaspoons salt
2 tablespoons sugar
2 tablespoons butter, melted

1. Combine the flours and mix well. To make the working culture, mix the liquid culture with 1 cup of the flour mixture and ¼ cup of the beer in a large mixing bowl. Proof 12 hours at room temperature (68° to 72°) or 6 hours in a proofing box at 85°.

2. Mix and knead 1 cup of the flour mixture and ½ cup of the beer into the culture. Proof 8 hours at room temperature or 4 hours in the proofing box. After proofing, this is the fully active culture.

3. Punch down. Mix together the salt, sugar, butter, and the remaining ½ cup beer. Add to the dough and mix well. Reserve 1 cup of the flour mixture for flouring the board. Mix and spoon knead the remaining 1¾ cups flour mixture into the dough 1 cup at a time. When too stiff to mix by hand, transfer to the floured board and knead in the remaining flour.

4. Form 2 pan loaves, and proof at the same temperature used above until the dough rises about 1 inch above the pan tops (2½ to 3 hours).

5. Bake in a preheated oven at 375° for 40 to 45 minutes. Remove from the pans and cool on wire racks.

LIGHT SWEDISH LIMPA I

RECIPE WITH **LIQUID** CULTURE   Makes two 1½-pound loaves

Limpa is a rye bread flavored with brown sugar or molasses. This recipe uses brown sugar, but many of the Austrian limpas use both. The orange zest is an absolute requirement to complement the light rye flavor. Use a coarse grater to produce substantial strips and chunks of the zest. I bake this bread in loaf pans, but it can be formed into French loaves. Here are two ways to make one of my favorite recipes.

3¼ cups white flour
1 cup rye flour
2 cups cold liquid culture
1 cup water
1 teaspoon salt
½ cup firmly packed brown
  sugar

2 tablespoons butter
Grated zest of 1 orange
1 tablespoon caraway seeds
2 tablespoons fennel seeds

1. Combine the flours and mix well. To make the working culture, mix the liquid culture with 1 cup of the flour mixture and ¼ cup of the water in a large mixing bowl. Proof 12 hours at room temperature (68° to 72°) or 6 hours in a proofing box at 85°.

2. Add 1 cup of the flour mixture and ¼ cup of the water. Mix and knead until smooth. Proof 8 hours at room temperature or 4 hours in the proofing box. After proofing, this is the fully active culture.

3. Punch down. Dissolve the salt and brown sugar in the remaining ½ cup water. Add the butter and warm briefly to melt, then add the orange zest and caraway and fennel seeds. Add to the dough and mix well. Reserve 1 cup of the flour mixture for flouring the board. Mix and spoon knead the remaining 1¼ cups flour mixture into the dough 1 cup at a time. When too stiff to mix, transfer to the floured board and knead in the remaining flour.

4. Form 2 pan loaves, and proof at the same temperature used above until the dough rises about 1 inch above the pan tops (3 to 4 hours).

5. Bake in a preheated oven at 375° for 40 to 45 minutes. Remove from the pans and cool on wire racks.

LIGHT SWEDISH LIMPA II

RECIPE WITH **SPONGE** CULTURE   Makes two 1¹/₂-pound loaves

4¼ cups white flour	½ cup firmly packed brown sugar
1 cup rye flour	2 tablespoons butter
½ cup cold sponge culture	Grated zest of 1 orange
2 cups water	1 tablespoon caraway seeds
1 teaspoon salt	2 tablespoons fennel seeds

1. Combine the flours and mix well. To make the working culture, mix the sponge culture with 1½ cups of the flour mixture and ¾ cup of the water in a large mixing bowl. This is a very stiff mixture. Proof 12 hours at room temperature (68° to 72°) or 6 hours in a proofing box at 85°.

2. Add 1 cup of the flour mixture and ½ cup of the water. Mix and knead until smooth. Proof 8 hours at room temperature or 4 hours in the proofing box. After proofing, this is the fully active culture.

3. Punch down. Dissolve the salt and brown sugar in the remaining ¾ cup water. Add the butter and warm briefly to melt, then add the orange zest and caraway and fennel seeds. Add to the dough and mix well. Reserve 1 cup of the flour mixture for flouring the board. Mix and spoon knead the remaining 1¾ cups flour mixture into the dough 1 cup at a time. When too stiff to mix, transfer to the floured board and knead in the remaining flour.

4. Form loaves, proof, bake, and cool as directed for Recipe I.

OATMEAL BREAD

RECIPE WITH **SPONGE** CULTURE   Makes two 1¹/₂-pound loaves

This recipe produces an interesting variation on sourdough bread. It is somewhat rougher in texture but rises well. I have also tried this recipe with steel-cut oats.

4 cups white flour	*1 cup milk*
2 cups rolled oats	*1½ teaspoons salt*
½ cup cold sponge culture	*2 tablespoons firmly packed*
1¼ cups water	*brown sugar*

1. Combine the flour and rolled oats and mix well. To make the working culture, mix the sponge culture with 1½ cups of the flour mixture and 1 cup of the water in a large mixing bowl. Proof 12 hours at room temperature (68° to 72°) or 6 hours in a proofing box.

2. Add 1 cup of the flour mixture and ¼ cup of the water. Mix and knead until smooth. Proof 12 hours at room temperature or 6 hours in the proofing box. After proofing, this is your fully active culture.

3. Punch down. Mix together the milk, salt, and brown sugar. Add to the dough and mix well. Reserve 1 cup of the flour mixture for flouring the board. Mix and spoon knead the remaining 2½ cups flour mixture into the dough 1 cup at a time. When too stiff to mix by hand, transfer to the floured board and knead in the remaining flour mixture.

4. Form 2 pan loaves or French loaves, and proof them at the same temperature used above until ready to bake (2½ to 4 hours).

5. Bake in a preheated oven at 375° for 40 to 45 minutes. Remove from the pans and cool on wire racks.

ONION-OLIVE BREAD

RECIPE WITH **LIQUID** CULTURE   Makes one 2-pound loaf

This is a delicious bread originally from Greece and Cyprus. I like to use our Bahrain culture with this recipe.

2 cups liquid culture	*1 tablespoon olive oil, plus*
3½ cups white flour	*oil for brushing*
½ cup water	*1 cup chopped black olives*
1 onion, finely chopped	*1 teaspoon salt*

1. Mix the liquid culture with 1 cup of flour in a large mixing bowl. This is the working culture. Proof 12 hours at room temperature (68° to 72°) or 6 hours in a proofing box at 85°.

2. Add 1 cup of the flour and ¼ cup of the water. Mix and knead until smooth. Proof 8 hours at room temperature or 4 hours in the proofing box. After proofing, this is the fully active culture.

3. In a skillet, sauté the onion in the 1 tablespoon olive oil for about 2 to 5 minutes, until translucent. Remove the skillet from the heat, add the olives, and let cool.

4. Punch down the dough. Dissolve the salt in the remaining ¼ cup water. Add to the dough and mix well. Reserve 1 cup of the flour for the board. Mix and spoon knead the remaining ½ cup flour into the dough. When too stiff to mix by hand, transfer to the floured board and knead in the remaining flour.

5. Flatten the dough by hand and with a rolling pin into a rectangle about 6 by 9 inches and ½ inch thick.

6. Spread the onion-olive mix over the surface of the dough, leaving a 1-inch border uncovered on all sides. Roll up from a long side into a loaf. Pinch ends to seal.

7. Place on a baking sheet, cover lightly with plastic wrap, and proof 2 hours at room temperature or 1 hour at 85°.

8. Make several diagonal slashes in the top of the loaf with a sharp edge. Brush with olive oil.

9. Bake in a preheated oven at 375° for 45 to 50 minutes. Cool on a wire rack.

POTATO BREAD

RECIPE WITH **LIQUID** CULTURE   Makes two 1½-pound loaves

Prepared instant mashed potatoes (1 cup) may be substituted for the boiled potatoes. The addition of either gives this hearty white bread a distinctive flavor and texture. Many of the older sourdough bakers fed their starters with boiled potatoes, which is not a good idea at all as it may cause bacteria growth. Here, the addition is primarily for flavor. Naturally, I use my homegrown Idaho spuds.

½ cup cold liquid culture	1½ teaspoons salt
6 cups flour	2 tablespoons butter, melted
1 cup water	2 potatoes, boiled and
1 cup milk	mashed (1 cup)

1. Mix the liquid culture with 1 cup of the flour and ½ cup of the water in a large mixing bowl. Proof 12 hours at room temperature (68° to 72°) or 6 hours in a proofing box at 85°.

2. Add 1 cup of the flour and ½ cup of the water. Mix and knead until smooth. Proof 8 hours at room temperature or 4 hours in the proofing box. After proofing, this is the fully active culture.

3. Punch down. Mix together the milk, salt, butter, and mashed potatoes. Add to the dough and mix well. Reserve 1 cup of the flour for flouring the board. Mix and spoon knead the remaining 3 cups flour into the dough 1 cup at a time. When too stiff to mix by hand, transfer to the floured board and knead in the remaining flour.

4. Form 2 pan loaves or French loaves, and proof them at the same temperature used above until ready to bake (3 to 4 hours).

5. Bake in a preheated oven at 375° for 40 to 45 minutes. Remove from the pans and cool on wire racks.

PUMPERNICKEL RYE BREAD

RECIPE WITH **LIQUID** CULTURE   Makes two 1½-pound loaves

Pumpernickel is a coarsely ground rye flour with poor or no gluten, so it does not rise well. It does produce a moist, dark bread ideal for buffets, however. I have used Vital Gluten in this recipe with good results.

2 cups coarse pumpernickel flour	1½ teaspoons salt
2¾ cups white flour	2 tablespoons sugar
2 cups cold liquid culture	1 cup milk
¾ cup water	1 tablespoon caraway seeds
	2 tablespoons vegetable oil

1. Combine the flours and mix well. Mix the liquid culture with 1 cup of the flour mixture and ¼ cup of water in a large mixing bowl. This is the working culture. Proof 12 hours at room temperature (68° to 72°) or 6 hours in a proofing box at 85°.

2. Add and mix 1 cup of the flour mixture and the remaining ½ cup water. Mix and knead until smooth. Proof 8 hours at room temperature or 4 hours in the proofing box. After proofing, this is the fully active culture.

3. Punch down. Dissolve the salt and sugar in the milk and add the caraway seeds and oil. Add to the dough and mix well. Reserve 1 cup of the flour mixture for flouring the board. Mix and spoon knead the remaining 1¾ cups flour mixture into the dough 1 cup at a time. When too stiff to mix by hand, transfer to the floured board and knead in the remaining flour.

4. Divide the dough in half, form into balls, and then flatten into 2-inch-thick rounds. Fold over once to form oval loaves. Pinch seams to seal.

5. Place on a baking sheet, seam side down, cover with light plastic wrap, and proof until ready to bake (2½ to 3 hours).

6. Bake in a preheated oven at 400° for 55 to 60 minutes. Cool on wire racks.

RAISIN BRAN CEREAL SOURDOUGH

RECIPE WITH **LIQUID** CULTURE   Makes two 1¹/₂-pound loaves

This is a quick and easy way to put together a raisin bran sourdough right from what you have on your pantry shelf. I made this one with Kellogg's brand cereal, but there are others that will work just as well.

2 cups cold liquid culture	*1½ teaspoon salt*
4¾ cups flour	*1 tablespoon sugar*
1¼ cups water	*2 cups raisin bran cereal*

1. Mix the liquid culture with 1 cup of the flour and ¼ cup of the water in a large mixing bowl. This is the working culture. Proof 12 hours at room temperature (68° to 72°) or 6 hours in a proofing box at 85°.

2. Add 1 cup of the flour and ¼ cup of the water. Mix and knead until smooth. Proof 8 hours at room temperature or 4 hours in the proofing box. After proofing, this is the fully active culture.

3. Punch down. Mix together the salt, sugar, dry cereal, and the remaining ¾ cup water. Add to the dough and mix well. Reserve 1 cup of the flour for flouring the board. Mix and spoon knead the remaining 1¾ cups flour into the dough 1 cup at a time. When too stiff to mix by hand, transfer to the floured board and knead in the remaining flour.

4. Form 2 pan loaves, and proof at the same temperature used above until the dough rises about 1 inch above the pan tops (2½ to 3 hours).

5. Bake in a preheated oven at 375° for 40 to 45 minutes. Remove from the pans and cool on wire racks.

RAISIN RYE BREAD

RECIPE WITH **LIQUID** CULTURE   Makes two 1½-pound loaves

This makes great breakfast toast. For variety, substitute whole-wheat flour for the rye and use 2 tablespoons brown sugar instead of granulated sugar.

2 cups rye flour	*1 tablespoon sugar*
2¾ cups white flour	*1 tablespoon oil*
2 cups cold liquid culture	*2 cups raisins, plumped*
1¼ cups water	*(see Note)*
1½ teaspoons salt	

1. Combine the flours and mix well. To make the working culture, mix the liquid culture with 1 cup of the flour mixture and ¼ cup of the water in a large mixing bowl. Proof 12 hours at room temperature (68° to 72°) or 6 hours in a proofing box at 85°.

2. Add 1 cup of the flour mixture and ½ cup of the water. Mix and knead until smooth. Proof 8 hours at room temperature or 4 hours in the proofing box. After proofing, this is the fully active culture.

3. Punch down. Dissolve the salt and sugar in the remaining ½ cup water and add the oil and raisins. Add to the dough and mix well. Reserve 1 cup of the flour mixture for flouring the board. Mix and spoon knead the remaining 1¾ cups flour mixture into the dough 1 cup at a time. When too stiff to mix by hand, transfer to the floured board and knead in the remaining flour.

4. Form 2 pan loaves, and proof at the same temperature used above until the dough rises about 1 inch above the pan tops (2½ to 3 hours).

5. Bake in a preheated oven at 375° for 40 to 45 minutes. Remove from the pans and cool on wire racks.

≈ *Note:* To plump raisins, soak them in water to cover for 30 minutes, or place in water to cover and microwave on high for 1 minute. Cool and drain before adding to dough.

ROSEMARY BREAD

RECIPE WITH **LIQUID** CULTURE   Makes one 2-pound loaf

Instead of using dried rosemary in this Italian Easter bread, lightly brown 1 tablespoon chopped fresh rosemary in the olive oil, then discard the rosemary and let the oil cool before working it into the dough.

½ cup cold liquid culture	1 tablespoon sugar
3¾ cups white flour	1 teaspoon dried rosemary,
½ cup water	ground
¾ cup milk	½ cup raisins
¼ cup olive oil	3 eggs
1 teaspoon salt	

1. Mix the liquid culture with 1 cup of the flour and ¼ cup of the water in a large mixing bowl. This is the working culture. Proof 12 hours at room temperature (68° to 72°) or 6 hours in a proofing box at 85°.

2. Add 1 cup of the flour and the remaining ¼ cup water. Mix and knead until smooth. Proof 8 hours at room temperature or 4 hours in the proofing box. After proofing, this is the fully active culture.

3. Punch down. Mix together the milk, olive oil, salt, sugar, rosemary, and raisins. Lightly beat 2 of the eggs and add to the milk mixture. Add the milk mixture to the dough and mix well. Reserve 1 cup of the flour for flouring the board. Mix and spoon knead the remaining ¾ cup flour into the dough. When too stiff to mix by hand, transfer to the floured board and knead in any remaining flour.

4. Form an oval or round loaf, place on a baking sheet, cover lightly with plastic wrap, and proof until ready to bake (2 to 3 hours).

5. Make a crisscross slash in the top of the loaf with a sharp edge. Lightly beat the remaining egg and brush on the top of the loaf.

6. Bake in a preheated oven at 375° for 45 to 50 minutes. Remove from the baking sheet and cool on a wire rack.

SEVEN-GRAIN-CEREAL SOURDOUGH

RECIPE WITH **LIQUID** CULTURE   Makes two 1½-pound loaves

Several multigrain dry breakfast cereals are on the market, and they make great ingredients for sourdough breads. For this recipe I used Old Fashioned 7-Grain Cereal from the Montana Wheat Farms & Bakery in Three Forks, Montana. The seven grains are hard wheat, soft wheat, oats, rye, triticale, millet, and barley. All of them have gone through a roller process and are flattened. This is an easy way to complete a good recipe that otherwise might be a little difficult.

> *2 cups cold liquid culture*
> *4¾ cups flour*
> *1¼ cups water*
>
> *1½ teaspoons salt*
> *1½ cups multigrain dry cereal*

1. Mix the liquid culture with 1 cup of the flour and ¼ cup of the water in a large mixing bowl. This is the working culture. Proof 12 hours at room temperature (68° to 72°) or 6 hours in a proofing box at 85°.

2. Add 1 cup of the flour and ¼ cup of the water. Mix and knead until smooth. Proof 8 hours at room temperature or 4 hours in the proofing box. After proofing, this is the fully active culture.

3. Punch down. Mix together the remaining ¾ cup water, the salt, and the cereal. Add to the dough and mix well. Reserve 1 cup of the flour for flouring the board. Mix and spoon knead the remaining 1¾ cups flour into the dough 1 cup at a time. When too stiff to mix by hand, transfer to the floured board and knead in the remaining flour.

4. Form 2 pan loaves, and proof at the same temperature used above until the dough rises about 1 inch above the pan tops (2½ to 3 hours).

5. Bake in a preheated oven at 375° for 40 to 45 minutes. Remove from the pans and cool on wire racks.

SOUR CREAM RYE BREAD

RECIPE WITH **SPONGE** CULTURE   Makes two 1½-pound loaves

This is a heavy rye dough that will rise slowly, so consider using gluten flour if the dough doesn't rise enough the first time you make it. With an aggressive Russian culture, you may not need it. If you do need to use the gluten flour, see the directions on the container.

4 cups rye flour	2 teaspoons salt
2 cups white flour	4 teaspoons sugar
½ cup cold sponge culture	2 tablespoons vegetable oil
1¼ cups water	2 tablespoons caraway seeds
1 cup sour cream	

1. Combine the flours and mix well. To make the working culture, mix the sponge culture with 1½ cups of the flour mixture and 1 cup of the water in a large mixing bowl. Proof 12 hours at room temperature (68° to 72°) or 6 hours in a proofing box at 85°.

2. Add 1 cup of the flour mixture and the remaining ¼ cup water. Mix and knead until smooth. Proof 12 hours at room temperature or 6 hours in the proofing box. After proofing, this is the fully active culture.

3. Punch down. Mix together the sour cream, salt, sugar, oil, and caraway seeds. Add to the dough and mix well. Reserve 1 cup of the flour mixture for flouring the board. Mix and spoon knead the remaining 2½ cups flour mixture into the dough 1 cup at a time. When too stiff to mix by hand, transfer to the floured board and knead in the remaining flour.

4. Form 2 pan loaves or French loaves, and proof them at the same temperature used above until ready to bake (2½ to 4 hours).

5. Bake in a preheated oven at 375° for 40 to 45 minutes. Remove from the pans and cool on wire racks.

SUNFLOWER BREAD

RECIPE WITH **SPONGE** CULTURE   Makes two 1¹/₂-pound loaves

Sunflower seeds can be either raw, as in this recipe, or roasted. I much prefer
them raw.

3 cups whole-wheat flour	1 cup milk
3 cups white flour	1½ teaspoons salt
½ cup cold sponge culture	½ cup honey
1¼ cups water	1 cup raw sunflower seeds

1. Combine the flours and mix well. To make the working culture, mix the
    sponge culture with 1½ cups of the flour mixture and 1 cup of the water
    in a large mixing bowl. Proof 12 hours at room temperature (68° to 72°)
    or 6 hours in a proofing box at 85°.

2. Add 1 cup of the flour mixture and ¼ cup of the water. Mix and knead
    until smooth. Proof 12 hours at room temperature or 6 hours in the
    proofing box. After proofing, this is the fully active culture.

3. Punch down. Mix together the milk, salt, honey, and sunflower seeds.
    Add to the dough and mix well. Reserve 1 cup of the flour mixture for
    flouring the board. Mix and spoon knead the remaining 2½ cups flour
    mixture into the dough 1 cup at a time. When too stiff to mix by hand,
    transfer to the floured board and knead in the remaining flour.

4. Form 2 pan loaves or French loaves, and proof them at the same temper-
    ature used above until ready to bake (2½ to 4 hours).

5. Bake in a preheated oven at 375° for 40 to 45 minutes. Remove from the
    pans and cool on wire racks.

TANYA'S PEASANT BLACK BREAD

RECIPE WITH **LIQUID** CULTURE   Makes two 1½-pound loaves

My friend Tanya says this recipe really doesn't duplicate the bread of her native Russia, and I may yet have to go to her homeland to discover the secret ingredients of Russian bakers. The combination of coriander and molasses complements the sourdough flavor, so don't leave either out.

1 cup rye flour	*1 teaspoon salt*
1 cup whole-wheat flour	*½ cup milk*
1¼ cups white flour	*2 tablespoons dark molasses*
2 cups cold liquid culture	*2 tablespoons vegetable oil*
½ cup water	*1 teaspoon coriander*

1. Combine the flours and mix well. To make the working culture, mix the liquid culture with 1 cup of the flour mixture and ¼ cup of the water in a large mixing bowl. Proof 12 hours at room temperature (68° to 72°) or 6 hours in a proofing box at 85°.

2. Add 1 cup of the flour mixture and the remaining ¼ cup water. Mix and knead until smooth. Proof 8 hours at room temperature or 4 hours in the proofing box. After proofing, this is the fully active culture.

3. Punch down. Dissolve the salt in the milk and mix in the molasses, oil, and coriander. Add to the dough and mix well. Reserve 1 cup of the flour mixture for flouring the board. Mix and spoon knead the remaining ¼ cup flour mixture into the dough. When too stiff to mix by hand, transfer to the floured board and knead in the remaining flour.

4. Form 2 pan loaves, and proof at the same temperature used above until the dough rises about 1 inch above the pan tops (2½ to 3 hours).

5. Bake in a preheated oven at 375° for 40 to 45 minutes. Remove from the pans and cool on wire racks.

THE DO-GOOD LOAF

RECIPE WITH SPONGE CULTURE   Makes two 1½-pound loaves

This recipe was developed by my mentor, Dr. Clive McCay, at Cornell University in the 1940s when he was asked to improve the diet at New York State Mental Hospitals. It was dubbed the Do-Good Loaf by Jean Hewitt in the *New York Times Sunday Magazine*. Dr. McCay didn't make it with a sourdough culture, and it appears here because his student knows he would approve.

½ cup cold sponge culture	*2 tablespoons brown sugar*
6 cups white flour	*2 tablespoons vegetable oil*
2¼ cups water	*1½ tablespoons wheat germ*
½ cup nonfat dry milk	*½ cup full-fat soy flour*
1½ teaspoons salt	

1. Mix the sponge culture with 1½ cups of the flour and 1 cup of the water in a large mixing bowl. This is the working culture. Proof 12 hours at room temperature (68° to 72°) or 6 hours in a proofing box at 85°.

2. Add 1 cup of the flour and ¼ cup of the water. Mix and knead until smooth. Proof 12 hours at room temperature or 6 hours in the proofing box. After proofing, this is your fully active culture.

3. Punch down. Mix the remaining 1 cup water with the dry milk, salt, brown sugar, oil, wheat germ, and soy flour. Add to the dough and mix well. Reserve 1 cup of the flour for flouring the board. Mix and spoon knead the remaining 2½ cups flour into the dough 1 cup flour at a time. When too stiff to mix by hand, transfer to the floured board and knead in the remaining flour.

4. Form 2 pan or French loaves, and proof them at the same temperature used above until ready to bake (2½ to 4 hours).

5. Bake in a preheated oven at 375° for 40 to 45 minutes. Remove from the pans and cool on wire racks.

WHOLE-WHEAT BREAD

RECIPE WITH **LIQUID** CULTURE   Makes two 1¹/₂-pound loaves

Bob Linville, a good friend, calls this loaf one of his favorites. It has great flavor and texture. He uses our fast Russian culture to leaven this moderately heavy dough.

2 cups whole-wheat flour	*2 teaspoons salt*
2¾ cups white flour	*1 cup warm milk*
2 cups cold liquid culture	*2 tablespoons sugar*
¾ cup water	*2 tablespoons butter, melted*

1. Combine the flours and mix well. To make the working culture, mix the liquid culture with 1 cup of the flour mixture and ¼ cup of the water in a large mixing bowl. Proof 12 hours at room temperature (68° to 72°) or 6 hours in a proofing box at 85°.

2. Add 1 cup of the flour mixture and the remaining ½ cup water. Mix and knead until smooth. Proof 8 hours at room temperature or 4 hours in the proofing box. After proofing, this is the fully active culture.

3. Punch down. Dissolve the salt in the milk and mix in the sugar and butter. Add to the dough and mix well. Reserve 1 cup of the flour mixture for flouring the board. Mix and spoon knead the remaining 1¾ cups flour mixture into the dough 1 cup at a time. When too stiff to mix by hand, transfer to the floured board and knead in the remaining flour.

4. Form 2 pan loaves, and proof at the same temperature used above until the dough rises about 1 inch above the pan tops (2½ to 3 hours).

5. Bake in a preheated oven at 375° for 40 to 45 minutes. Remove from the pans and cool on wire racks.

RECIPES USING
SPECIAL FLOURS

Durum Recipes

You can use durum as a complete substitute for whole-wheat flours in any recipe in this book. Just be sure to review the information about the qualities of durum on pages 17 and 18. As with any whole-wheat flour, better leavening will occur with about 50 percent white flour, but I have successfully used durum with only 25 percent white flour. The flavor of durum is hard to resist.

DURUM RYE BREAD

RECIPE WITH **SPONGE** CULTURE   Makes two 1½-pound loaves

I've raved about the taste of durum in bread, but you'll think I've understated it when you try this recipe.

2 cups durum flour	*2 teaspoons salt*
3 cups white flour	*¼ cup firmly packed brown*
1 cup rye flour	*sugar*
½ cup cold sponge culture	*2 tablespoons butter, melted,*
1¼ cups water	*or oil*
1 cup milk	

1. Combine the flours and mix well. To make the working culture, mix the sponge culture with 1½ cups of the flour mixture and 1 cup of the water in a large mixing bowl. Proof 12 hours at room temperature (68° to 72°) or 6 hours in a proofing box at 85°.

2. Add 1 cup of the flour mixture and the remaining ¼ cup water. Mix and knead until smooth. Proof 12 hours at room temperature or 6 hours in the proofing box. After proofing, this is the fully active culture.

3. Punch down. Mix together the milk, salt, brown sugar, and butter. Add to the dough and mix well. Reserve 1 cup of the flour mixture for flouring the board. Mix and spoon knead the remaining 2½ cups flour mixture into the dough 1 cup at a time. When too stiff to mix by hand, transfer to the floured board and knead in the remaining flour.

4. Form 2 pan or French loaves, and proof them at the same temperature used above until ready to bake (2½ to 4 hours).

5. Bake in a preheated oven at 375° for 40 to 45 minutes. Remove from the pans and cool on wire racks.

DURUM SUNFLOWER BREAD

RECIPE WITH **SPONGE** CULTURE — Makes two 1½-pound loaves

This recipe results in a somewhat heavier loaf than the Durum Rye Bread (page 95). You may want to use the Russian culture to help this loaf along.

2 cups whole-wheat flour
2 cups durum flour
2 cups white flour
½ cup cold sponge culture
1¼ cups water
1 cup milk

2 teaspoons salt
½ cup honey
1 cup raw sunflower seeds
2 tablespoons butter, melted,
  or vegetable oil

1. Combine the flours and mix well. To make the working culture, mix the sponge culture with 1½ cups of the flour mixture and 1 cup of the water in a large mixing bowl. Proof 12 hours at room temperature (68° to 72°) or 6 hours in a proofing box at 85°.

2. Add 1 cup of the flour mixture and the remaining ¼ cup water. Mix and knead until smooth. Proof 12 hours at room temperature or 6 hours in the proofing box. After proofing, this is the fully active culture.

3. Punch down. Mix together the milk, salt, honey, sunflower seeds, and butter. Add to the dough and mix well. Reserve 1 cup of the flour mixture for flouring the board. Mix and spoon knead the remaining 2½ cups flour mixture into the dough 1 cup at a time. When too stiff to mix by hand, transfer to the floured board and knead in the remaining flour mixture.

4. Form 2 pan loaves or French loaves, and proof them at the same temperature used above until ready to bake (2½ to 4 hours).

5. Bake in a preheated oven at 375° for 40 to 45 minutes. Remove from pans and cool on wire racks.

DURUM WORLD BREAD

RECIPE WITH **SPONGE** CULTURE   Makes two 1½-pound loaves

Use this recipe to sample the unique taste of durum without masking the flavors of the other ingredients.

3 cups durum flour   *1 cup milk*
3 cups white flour   *1½ teaspoons salt*
½ cup cold sponge culture   *2 tablespoons sugar*
1¼ cups water   *1 tablespoon butter, melted*

1. Combine the flours and mix well. To make the working culture, mix the sponge culture with 1½ cups of the flour mixture and 1 cup of the water in a large mixing bowl. Proof 12 hours at room temperature (68° to 72°) or 6 hours in a proofing box at 85°.

2. Add 1 cup of the flour mixture and the remaining ¼ cup water. Mix and knead until smooth. Proof 12 hours at room temperature or 6 hours at 85°. After proofing, this is the fully active culture.

3. Punch down. Mix together the milk, salt, sugar, and butter. Add to the dough and mix well. Reserve 1 cup of the flour mixture for flouring the board. Mix and spoon knead the remaining 2½ cups flour mixture into the dough 1 cup at a time. When too stiff to mix by hand, transfer to the floured board and knead in the remaining flour mixture.

4. Form 2 pan loaves or French loaves, and proof them at the same temperature used above until ready to bake (2½ to 4 hours).

5. Bake in a preheated oven at 375° for 40 to 45 minutes. Remove from the pans and cool on wire racks.

DURUM SUNFLOWER BREAD WITH SOY

RECIPE WITH **SPONGE** CULTURE Makes two 1½-pound loaves

You may want to use our Russian culture to help along this somewhat heavy durum loaf.

1 cup soy flour	*1 cup milk*
2 cups durum flour	*2 teaspoons salt*
2 cups white flour	*½ cup honey*
1 cup whole-wheat flour	*1 cup raw sunflower seeds*
½ cup cold sponge culture	*2 tablespoons butter, melted,*
1¼ cups water	*or vegetable oil*

1. Combine the flours and mix well. To make the working culture, mix the sponge culture with 1½ cups of the flour mixture and 1 cup of the water in a large mixing bowl. Proof 12 hours at room temperature (68° to 72°) or 6 hours in a proofing box at 85°.

2. Add 1 cup of the flour mixture and the remaining ¼ cup water. Mix and knead until smooth. Proof 12 hours at room temperature or 6 hours in the proofing box. After proofing, this is the fully active culture.

3. Punch down. Mix together the milk, salt, honey, sunflower seeds, and butter. Add to the dough and mix well. Reserve 1 cup of the flour mixture for flouring the board. Mix and spoon knead the remaining 2½ cups flour mixture into the dough 1 cup at a time. When too stiff to mix by hand, transfer to the floured board and knead in the remaining flour mixture.

4. Form 2 pan or French loaves, and proof them at the same temperature used above until ready to bake (2½ to 4 hours).

5. Bake in a preheated oven at 375° for 40 to 45 minutes. Remove from the pans and cool in wire racks.

Flax Recipes

FLAX PRAIRIE BREAD

RECIPE WITH **LIQUID** CULTURE   Makes two 1½-pound loaves

This recipe comes right out of Manitoba flax country. When you need to increase your intake of omega-3 fatty acids and can't afford to eat salmon four times a week, this is a good substitute and much less expensive.

½ cup flax flour	3 tablespoons honey
4¼ cups flour	3 tablespoons vegetable oil
2 cups cold liquid culture	2 tablespoons sunflower seeds
1¼ cups water	¼ cup flaxseeds
1½ teaspoons salt	1 tablespoon poppyseeds

1. Combine the flours and mix well. To make the working culture, mix the liquid culture with 1 cup of the flour mixture and ¼ cup of the water in a large mixing bowl. Proof 12 hours at room temperature (68° to 72°) or 6 hours in a proofing box at 85°.

2. Add 1 cup of the flour mixture and ½ cup of the water. Mix and knead until smooth. Proof 8 hours at room temperature or 4 hours in the proofing box. After proofing, this is the fully active culture.

3. Punch down. Mix together the remaining ½ cup water, the salt, honey, oil, and all the seeds. Add to the dough and mix well. Reserve 1 cup of the flour mixture for flouring the board. Mix and spoon knead the remaining 1¾ cups flour mixture into the dough 1 cup at a time. When too stiff to mix by hand, transfer to the floured board and knead in the remaining flour mixture.

4. Form 2 pan loaves, and proof at same temperature used above until the dough rises about 1 inch above the pan tops (2½ to 3 hours).

5. Bake in a preheated oven at 375° for 40 to 45 minutes. Remove from the pans and cool on wire racks.

PUMPERNICKEL RYE BREAD WITH FLAX

RECIPE WITH **LIQUID** CULTURE   Makes two 1½-pound loaves

Pumpernickel is a coarsely ground rye flour with poor or no gluten, so it does not rise especially well. It does produce a moist, dark bread ideal for buffets, however. Here I have used whole flaxseeds, but flax flour can also be used.

*2 cups coarse pumpernickel
   flour
2¾ cups white flour
2 cups cold liquid culture
¾ cup water
1½ teaspoons salt*

*2 tablespoons sugar
1 cup milk
1 tablespoon caraway seeds
½ cup flaxseeds
2 tablespoons vegetable oil*

1. Combine the flours and mix well. To make the working culture, mix the liquid culture with 1 cup of the flour mixture and ¼ cup water in a large mixing bowl. Proof 12 hours at room temperature (68° to 72°) or 6 hours in a proofing box at 85°.

2. Add 1 cup of the flour mixture and the remaining ½ cup water. Proof 8 hours at room temperature or 4 hours in the proofing box. After proofing, this is the fully active culture.

3. Punch down. Dissolve the salt and sugar in the milk and add the caraway seeds, flaxseeds, and oil. Add to the dough and mix well. Reserve 1 cup of the flour mixture for flouring the board. Mix and spoon knead the remaining 1¾ cups remaining flour mixture into the dough 1 cup at a time. When too stiff to mix by hand, transfer to the floured board and knead in the remaining flour mixture.

4. Form 2 equal balls and flatten into 2-inch-thick rounds. Fold over once to form oval loaves. Pinch seams to seal. Place on a baking sheet, seam side down, and proof them at the same temperature used above until ready to bake (2½ to 3 hours).

5. Bake in a preheated oven at 400° for 55 to 60 minutes. Remove from the baking sheet and cool on wire racks.

WHOLE-WHEAT BREAD WITH FLAX

RECIPE WITH **LIQUID** CULTURE   Makes two 1½-pound loaves

This is a winner in both flavor and texture. We use our fast Russian culture to leaven this moderately heavy dough. This recipe uses flax flour. You could also substitute flaxseeds for the flour.

½ cup flax flour	*1¼ cups water*
2 cups whole-wheat flour	*2 teaspoons salt*
2¼ cups white flour	*2 tablespoons sugar*
2 cups cold liquid culture	*2 tablespoons butter, melted*

1. Combine the flours and mix well. To make the working culture, mix the liquid culture with 1 cup of the flour mixture and ¼ cup of the water in a large mixing bowl. Proof 12 hours at room temperature (68° to 72°) or 6 hours in a proofing box at 85°.

2. Add 1 cup of the flour mixture and ½ cup of the water. Mix and knead until smooth. Proof 8 hours at room temperature or 4 hours in the proofing box. After proofing, this is the fully active culture.

3. Punch down. Dissolve the salt and sugar in the remaining ½ cup water and mix with the butter. Add to the dough and mix well. Reserve 1 cup of the flour mixture for flouring the board. Mix and spoon knead the remaining 1¾ cups flour mixture into the dough 1 cup at a time. When too stiff to mix by hand, transfer to the floured board and knead in the remaining flour mixture.

4. Form 2 pan loaves, and proof at the same temperature used above until the dough is about 1 inch above the pan tops (2½ to 3 hours).

5. Bake in a preheated oven at 375° for 40 to 45 minutes. Remove from the pans and cool on wire racks.

Spelt Recipes

HERB SPELT BREAD

RECIPE WITH **LIQUID** CULTURE   Makes two 1½-pound loaves

This recipe, which uses only white spelt flour, enables you to compare the leavening characteristics and flavor of spelt with those of wheat flours.

2 cups cold liquid culture	*1½ teaspoons salt*
4¾ cups white spelt flour	*1 tablespoon sugar*
½ cup water	*1 teaspoon dried thyme*
¾ cup milk	*1 teaspoon dried oregano*
2 tablespoons butter, melted	*1 teaspoon dried basil*

1. Mix the liquid culture with 1 cup of the flour and ¼ cup of the water in a large mixing bowl. This is the working culture. Proof 12 hours at room temperature (68° to 72°) or 6 hours in a proofing box at 85°.

2. Add 1 cup of the flour and the remaining ¼ cup water. Mix and knead until smooth. Proof 8 hours at room temperature or 4 hours in the proofing box. After proofing, this is the fully active culture.

3. Punch down. Mix together the milk, butter, salt, sugar, and dried herbs. Add to the dough and mix well. Reserve 1 cup of the flour for flouring the board. Mix and spoon knead the remaining 1¾ cups flour into the dough 1 cup at a time. When too stiff to mix by hand, transfer to the floured board and knead in the remaining flour.

4. Form 2 pan loaves, and proof at the same temperature used above until the dough is about 1 inch above the pan tops (2½ to 3 hours).

5. Bake in a preheated oven at 375° for 40 to 45 minutes. Remove from the pans and cool on wire racks.

SPELT BREAD

RECIPE WITH **LIQUID** CULTURE   Makes two 1½-pound loaves

Spelt, like kamut, is an ancient grain, and both make excellent additions to many sourdough breads. This recipe is made with white and rye flours, but you may also use spelt in whole-wheat breads or as a substitute for rye in rye breads. This is a good recipe to compare the qualities of spelt and kamut.

1 cup white spelt flour	*1½ teaspoons salt*
1 cup rye flour	*2 tablespoons sugar*
2¾ cups white flour	*¼ cup vegetable oil*
2 cups cold liquid culture	*2 tablespoons caraway seeds*
1¼ cups water	

1. Combine the flours and mix well. To make the working culture, mix the liquid culture with 1 cup of the flour mixture and ¼ cup of the water in a large mixing bowl. Proof 12 hours at room temperature (68° to 72°) or 6 hours in a proofing box at 85°.

2. Add 1 cup of the flour mixture and ½ cup water. Mix and knead until smooth. Proof 8 hours at room temperature or 4 hours in the proofing box. After proofing, this is the fully active culture.

3. Punch down. Mix together the remaining ½ cup water, the salt, sugar, oil, and caraway seeds. Add to the dough and mix well. Reserve 1 cup of the flour mixture for flouring board. Mix and spoon knead the remaining 1¾ cups flour mixture into the dough 1 cup at a time. When too stiff to mix by hand, transfer to the floured board and knead in the remaining flour.

4. Form 2 pan loaves, and proof at the same temperature used above until the dough is about 1 inch above the pan tops (2½ to 3 hours).

5. Bake in a preheated oven at 375° for 40 to 45 minutes. Remove from the pans and cool on wire racks.

AUSTRIAN SPELT BREAD

RECIPE WITH **LIQUID** CULTURE   Makes two 1½-pound loaves

I make the spelt breads described in this book with organically grown spelt produced by Purity Foods under the label Vita-Spelt. This one, which contains molasses and brown sugar, has an exceptional flavor.

1 cup medium rye flour	*2 tablespoons firmly packed*
1 cup whole-wheat flour	*brown sugar*
2¾ cups white spelt flour	*2 tablespoons molasses*
2 cups cold liquid culture	*2 tablespoons vegetable oil*
1¼ cups water	*1 tablespoon caraway seeds*
1½ teaspoons salt	*2 tablespoons fennel seeds*

1. Combine the flours and mix well. To make the working culture, mix the liquid culture with 1 cup of the flour mixture and ¼ cup of the water in a large mixing bowl. Proof 12 hours at room temperature (68° to 72°) or 6 hours in a proofing box at 85°.

2. Add 1 cup of the flour mixture and ½ cup of the water. Mix and knead until smooth. Proof 8 hours at room temperature or 4 hours in the proofing box. After proofing, this is the fully active culture.

3. Punch down. Mix together the remaining ½ cup water, salt, brown sugar, molasses, oil, and all the seeds. Add to the dough and mix well. Reserve 1 cup of the flour mixture for flouring the board. Mix and spoon knead the remaining 1¾ cups flour mixture into the dough 1 cup at a time. When too stiff to mix by hand, transfer to floured board and knead in the remaining flour mixture.

4. Form 2 pan loaves, and proof at the same temperature used above until the dough is about 1 inch above the pan tops (2½ to 3 hours).

5. Bake in a preheated oven at 375° for 40 to 45 minutes. Remove from the pans and cool on wire racks.

CARAWAY SPELT BREAD

RECIPE WITH LIQUID CULTURE   Makes two 1½-pound loaves

Spelt produces a rich, creamy texture when added to a sourdough culture, and the physical difference between spelt flour and wheat flours is immediately obvious. The flavor of caraway with spelt is equally unique.

2 cups rye flour   *1½ teaspoons salt*
2¾ cups white spelt flour   *2 tablespoons butter, melted*
2 cups cold liquid culture   *2 tablespoons dark molasses*
1¼ cups water   *2 tablespoons caraway seeds*

1. Combine the flours and mix well. To make the working culture, mix the liquid culture with 1 cup of the flour mixture and ¼ cup of the water to liquid in a large mixing bowl. Proof 12 hours at room temperature (68° to 72°) or 6 hours in a proofing box at 85°.

2. Add 1 cup of the flour mixture and ½ cup of the water. Mix and knead until smooth. Proof 8 hours at room temperature or 4 hours in the proofing box. After proofing, this is the fully active culture.

3. Punch down. Mix together the remaining ½ cup water, the salt, butter, molasses, and caraway seeds. Add to the dough and mix well. Reserve 1 cup of the flour mixture for flouring the board. Mix and spoon knead the remaining 1¾ cups flour mixture into the dough 1 cup at a time. When too stiff to mix by hand, transfer to the floured board and knead in the remaining flour mixture.

4. Form 2 pan loaves, and proof at the same temperature used above until the dough rises about 1 inch above the pan tops (2½ to 3 hours).

5. Bake in a preheated oven at 375° for 40 to 45 minutes. Remove from the pans and cool on wire racks.

Soy Recipes

CARAWAY RYE BREAD WITH SOY

RECIPE WITH **LIQUID** CULTURE   Makes two 1½-pound loaves

Few ingredients make a better combination than caraway and rye. Although many of these recipes utilize caraway, this one particularly enhances the two flavors.

1 cup soy flour	*1½ teaspoons salt*
2 cups light rye flour	*¾ cup dark molasses*
2 cups white flour	*2 tablespoons butter, melted*
2 cups cold liquid culture	*2 tablespoons caraway seeds*
1½ cups water	

1. Combine the flours and mix well. To make the working culture, mix the liquid culture with 1 cup of the flour mixture and ¼ cup of the water in a large mixing bowl. Proof 12 hours at room temperature (68° to 72°) or 6 hours in a proofing box at 85°.

2. Add 1 cup of the flour mixture and ½ cup of the water. Mix and knead until smooth. Proof 8 hours at room temperature or 4 hours in the proofing box. After proofing, this is the fully active culture.

3. Punch down. Mix together the remaining ¾ cup water, the salt, molasses, butter, and caraway seeds. Add to the dough and mix well. Reserve 1 cup of the flour mixture for flouring the board. Mix and spoon knead the remaining 2 cups flour mixture into the dough 1 cup at a time. When too stiff to mix by hand, transfer to the floured board and knead in the remaining flour mixture.

4. Form 2 pan loaves, and proof at the same temperature used above until the dough rises about 1 inch above the pan tops (2½ to 3 hours).

5. Bake in a preheated oven at 400° for 45 to 50 minutes. Remove from the pans and cool on wire racks.

DURUM SUNFLOWER BREAD WITH SOY

RECIPE WITH **SPONGE** CULTURE   Makes two 1¹/₂-pound loaves

This is a somewhat heavier durum recipe. You may want to use the Russian culture to help it along.

1 cup whole-wheat flour	*1 cup milk*
1 cup soy flour	*2 teaspoons salt*
2 cups durum flour	*2 tablespoons butter, melted,*
2 cups white flour	*or vegetable oil*
½ cup cold sponge culture	*½ cup honey*
1¼ cups water	*1 cup raw sunflower seeds*

1. Combine the flours and mix well. To make the working culture, mix the sponge culture with 1½ cups of the flour mixture and 1 cup of the water in a large mixing bowl. Proof 12 hours at room temperature (68° to 72°) or 6 hours in a proofing box at 85°.

2. Add 1 cup of the flour mixture and the remaining ¼ cup water. Mix and knead until smooth. Proof 12 hours at room temperature or 6 hours in the proofing box. After proofing, this is the fully active culture.

3. Punch down. Mix together the milk, salt, butter, honey, and sunflower seeds. Add to the dough and mix well. Reserve 1 cup of the flour mixture for flouring the board. Mix and spoon knead the remaining 2½ cups flour mixture into the dough 1 cup at a time. When too stiff to mix by hand, transfer to the floured board and knead in the remaining flour mixture.

4. Form 2 pan or French loaves, and proof them at the same temperature used above until ready to bake (2½ to 4 hours).

5. Bake in a preheated oven at 375° for 40 to 45 minutes. Remove from the pans and cool on wire racks.

WORLD BREAD WITH SOY

RECIPE WITH **LIQUID** CULTURE   Makes two 1½-pound loaves

An almost infinite number of soy flours are available, from full fat to nonfat to refatted, to name but a few. Your choice will be limited to what is available in your locality, of course, but you should try whatever you find on the shelf.

½ cup soy flour	¾ cup milk
4¾ cups flour	1½ teaspoons salt
2 cups cold liquid culture	2 tablespoons sugar
½ cup water	2 tablespoons butter, melted

1. Combine the flours and mix well. To make the working culture, mix the liquid culture with 1 cup of the flour mixture and ¼ cup of the water in a large mixing bowl. Proof 12 hours at room temperature (68° to 72°) or 6 hours in a proofing box at 85°.

2. Add 1 cup of the flour mixture and the remaining ¼ cup water. Mix and knead until smooth. Proof 8 hours at room temperature or 4 hours in the proofing box. After proofing, this is the fully active culture.

3. Punch down. Mix together the milk, salt, sugar, and butter. Add to the dough and mix well. Reserve 1 cup of the flour mixture for flouring the board. Mix and spoon knead the remaining 2¼ cups flour mixture into the dough 1 cup at a time. When too stiff to mix by hand, transfer to the floured board and knead in the remaining flour mixture.

4. Form 2 pan loaves, and proof at the same temperature used above until the dough rises about 1 inch above the pan tops (2½ to 3 hours).

5. Bake in a preheated oven at 375° for 40 to 45 minutes. Remove from the pans and cool on wire racks.

Kamut Recipe

KAMUT BREAD

RECIPE WITH **LIQUID** CULTURE   Makes two 1½-pound loaves

Kamut may or may not have originated in ancient Egypt. Agronomists are inclined to classify it as a subtype of durum. Whatever it is called or related to, it imparts a distinctive nutty flavor to a sourdough loaf. Its relationship to durum is perhaps an explanation for its relatively poor gluten content. It can be substituted for 1 cup rye or whole-wheat flour in any recipe. If you use more than 1 cup, it is a good idea to add a little gluten flour.

1 cup rye flour	*1½ teaspoons salt*
1 cup kamut flour	*2 tablespoons sugar*
2 cups white flour	*¼ cup vegetable oil*
2 cups cold liquid culture	*2 tablespoons caraway seeds*
1¼ cups water	

1. Combine the flours and mix well. To make the working culture, mix the liquid culture with 1 cup of the flour mixture and ¼ cup of the water in a large mixing bowl. Proof 12 hours at room temperature (68° to 72°) or 6 hours in a proofing box at 85°.

2. Add 1 cup of the flour mixture and ½ cup of the water. Mix and knead until smooth. Proof 8 hours at room temperature or 4 hours in the proofing box.

3. Punch down. Mix together the remaining ½ cup water, the salt, sugar, oil, and caraway seeds. Add to the dough and mix well. Reserve 1 cup of the flour mixture for flouring board. Mix and spoon knead the remaining 1 cup flour into the dough. When too stiff to mix by hand, transfer to the floured board and knead in the remaining flour mixture.

4. Form 2 pan loaves, and proof at the same temperature used above until the dough rises about 1 inch above the pan tops (2½ to 3 hours).

5. Bake in a preheated oven at 375° for 40 to 45 minutes. Remove from the pans and cool on wire racks.

Bulgur Recipes

BULGUR BREAD I

RECIPE WITH **LIQUID** CULTURE   Makes two 1½-pound loaves

Bulgur soaks up a lot of water, which makes it difficult to achieve a good dough consistency. Be prepared to add a little more water as you mix this dough, as exact amounts are hard to provide. Bulgur is sold in a granular form rather than as a flour, and it comes in several grades, from fine to extra coarse. This recipe was made with a medium no. 2 grade. You can add the bulgur either as an ingredient in the third step or as a portion of the flour in the first step. Here it is added as an ingredient.

2 cups cold liquid culture   *1½ teaspoon salt*
4½ cups white flour   *1 cup medium-grade bulgur*
2 cups water

1.   Mix the liquid culture with 1 cup of flour and ½ cup of the water in a large mixing bowl. This is the working culture. Proof 12 hours at room temperature (68° to 72°) or 6 hours in a proofing box at 85°.

2.   Add 1 cup of the flour and ½ cup of the water. Mix and knead until smooth. Proof 8 hours at room temperature or 4 hours in the proofing box. After proofing, this is the fully active culture.

3.   Punch down. Add the remaining 1 cup water, the salt, and the bulgur to the dough. Reserve 1 cup of the flour for flouring the board. Mix and spoon knead the remaining 1½ cups flour into the dough 1 cup at a time. When too stiff to mix by hand, transfer to the floured board and knead in the remaining flour.

4.   Form 2 pan loaves, and proof at the same temperature used above until the dough rises about 1 inch above the pan tops (2½ to 3 hours).

5.   Bake in a preheated oven at 375° for 40 to 45 minutes. Remove from the pans and cool on wire racks.

BULGUR BREAD II

RECIPE WITH **LIQUID** CULTURE   Makes two 1½-pound loaves

This recipe is exactly the same as Bulgur Bread I, but the bulgur is added as a portion of the flour. This produces a much longer fermentation of the bulgur granules and produces a somewhat different consistency. Both methods are good.

> *2 cups cold liquid culture*   *2 cups water*
> *4¾ cups flour*   *1½ teaspoons salt*
> *1 cup medium-grind bulgur*

1. Mix the liquid culture with 1 cup of the flour, the bulgur, and 1 cup of the water in a large mixing bowl. This is the working culture. Proof 12 hours at room temperature (68° to 72°) or 6 hours in a proofing box at 85°.

2. Add 1 cup of the flour and ½ cup of the water. Mix and knead until smooth. Proof 8 hours at room temperature or 4 hours in the proofing box. After proofing, this is the fully active culture.

3. Punch down. Dissolve the salt in the remaining ½ cup water. Add to the dough and mix well. Reserve 1 cup of the flour for flouring the board. Mix and spoon knead the remaining 1¾ cups flour into the dough 1 cup at a time. When too stiff to mix by hand, transfer to the floured board and knead in the remaining flour.

4. Form 2 pan loaves, and proof at the same temperature used above until the dough rises about 1 inch above the pan tops (2½ to 3 hours).

5. Bake in a preheated oven at 375° for 40 to 45 minutes. Remove from the pans and cool on wire racks.

WHOLE-GRAIN BULGUR BREAD

RECIPE WITH **LIQUID** CULTURE   Makes two 1½-pound loaves

You haven't really experienced bulgur until you've tried whole-grain bulgur. It can be used either raw or cooked, and I like it both ways. To cook it, I add 1 cup whole-grain bulgur to 2 cups boiling water and cook at low heat for 30 minutes or until tender. Then I drain off and retain the excess water, which I use as part of the water in the recipe. (Why waste all those vitamins and minerals?) During cooking, the bulgur kernels swell to more than double their volume, indicating that they have absorbed a lot of water. This results in a smaller amount of water needed for making the dough.

2 cups of cold liquid culture   *½ cup water*
4¾ cups flour   *1½ teaspoons salt*
1 cup whole-grain bulgur,
* cooked as above*

1. Mix the liquid culture with 1 cup of the flour and the cooked bulgur in a large mixing bowl. This is the working culture. Proof 12 hours at room temperature (68° to 72°) or 6 hours in a proofing box at 85°.

2. Add 1 cup of the flour and ¼ cup of the water. Mix and knead until smooth. Proof 8 hours at room temperature or 4 hours in the proofing box. After proofing, this is the fully active culture.

3. Punch down. Dissolve the salt in the remaining ¼ cup water. Add to the dough and mix well. Reserve 1 cup of the flour for flouring the board. Mix and spoon knead the remaining 1¾ cups flour into the dough 1 cup at a time. When too stiff to mix by hand, transfer to the floured board and knead in the remaining flour.

4. Form 2 pan loaves, and proof at the same temperature used above until the dough rises about 1 inch above the pan tops (2½ to 3 hours).

5. Bake in a preheated oven at 375° for 40 to 45 minutes. Remove from the pans and cool on wire racks.

SOURDOUGH SPECIALTIES

Everything in this section, from breadsticks to pizza to dinner rolls, comes with the special flavor of sourdough. By extending the proofing times, you can make wonderful snacks that your guests have never before tasted. Sourdough biscuits are almost as acclaimed as San Francisco bread, and the hamburger buns are satisfyingly unique. These are recipes for teaching your youngsters the fun of baking.

SOURDOUGH BAGELS

RECIPE WITH **LIQUID** CULTURE   Makes 15 bagels

You probably think you've eaten sourdough bagels somewhere, but unless you made them they probably weren't the real thing. You won't forget these.

2 cups cold liquid culture	*1 teaspoon salt*
4 cups white all-purpose flour	*4 tablespoons sugar*
½ cup plus 4 quarts water	*2 tablespoons vegetable oil*
½ cup milk	*2 eggs, beaten*

1. Mix the liquid culture with 1 cup of the flour and ¼ cup of the water in a large mixing bowl. This is the working culture. Proof 12 hours at room temperature (68° to 72°) or 6 hours in a proofing box at 85°.

2. Add 1 cup of flour and ¼ cup water. Mix and knead until smooth. Proof 8 hours at room temperature or 4 hours in the proofing box. After proofing, this is the fully active culture.

3. Punch down. Mix together the milk, the salt, 2 tablespoons of the sugar, the oil, and the eggs. Add to the dough and mix well. Reserve 1 cup of the flour for flouring the board. Mix and spoon knead the remaining 1 cup flour into the dough. When too stiff to work by hand, transfer to the floured board and knead in the remaining flour.

4. Divide the dough into 15 equal balls. Roll each ball into a 6-inch-long rope. Pinch the ends of each together to form a doughnut shape. Proof 2 hours at room temperature or 1 hour in the proofing box.

5. Bring the 4 quarts water to a boil in a large pot and add the remaining 2 tablespoons sugar. Drop the bagels, two at a time, into the boiling water. When they rise to the surface, using tongs or a slotted spoon, transfer to paper towels to drain briefly, then place on a baking sheet.

6. Bake in a preheated oven at 375° for 20 to 25 minutes, or until browned. Transfer the bagels to wire racks to cool.

BREADSTICKS

RECIPE WITH **LIQUID** CULTURE   Makes about 20 breadsticks, depending on size

You should pull and roll these sticks of dough until they reach the length you prefer. They can be as long and thin or as short and fat as you like. The thicker sticks are chewy, while the thinner ones are crisp. They freeze well in plastic freezer bags, and you can heat them in seconds in the microwave. A mixture of sticks, each coated with different seeds or with coarse salt, is delicious with cocktails or beer.

2 cups cold liquid culture   *1½ teaspoons salt*
4¾ cups flour   *1 tablespoon sugar*
1¼ cups water   *1 tablespoon butter, melted*

Glaze
2 eggs, beaten
Poppyseeds, sesame seeds, or
    coarse salt

1. Mix the liquid culture with 1 cup of the flour and ¼ cup of the water in a large mixing bowl. This is the working culture. Proof 12 hours at room temperature (68° to 72°) or 6 hours in a proofing box at 85°.

2. Add 1 cup of the flour and ½ cup of the water. Mix and knead until smooth. Proof 8 hours at room temperature or 4 hours at 85° in the proofing box. After proofing, this is the fully active culture.

3. Punch down. Mix together the remaining ½ cup water, salt, sugar, and butter. Add to the dough and mix well. Reserve 1 cup of the flour for flouring the board. Mix and spoon knead the remaining 1¾ cups into the dough 1 cup at a time. When too stiff to work by hand, transfer to the floured board and knead in the remaining flour.

4. Divide the dough into about 20 small balls. Roll each ball into a rope ¼ to ½ inch in diameter. Arrange the ropes 1 inch apart on a baking sheet. Proof at room temperature until they start to rise or 30 to 45 minutes in the proofing box.

5. To glaze the breadsticks, brush them with the eggs and sprinkle with the seeds.

6. Bake in a preheated oven at 375° for 15 to 20 minutes, or until uniformly brown. Transfer to wire racks to cool.

CARAWAY CRUNCHES

RECIPE WITH **LIQUID** CULTURE   Makes 16 crunches

These sourdough snacks will disappear in a hurry. You can easily double the recipe to make the supply last longer.

4¾ cups flour   *1½ teaspoons salt*
1¼ cups water   *1 tablespoon sugar*
2 cups cold liquid culture   *1 tablespoon butter, melted*

Glaze

2 eggs, beaten
2 tablespoons caraway seeds

1. Mix 1 cup of the flour and ¼ cup of the water with liquid culture in a large mixing bowl. This is the working culture. Proof 12 hours at room temperature (68° to 72°) or 6 hours in a proofing box at 85°.

2. Add 1 cup of the flour and ½ cup of the water. Mix and knead until smooth. Proof 8 hours at room temperature or 4 hours at 85° in the proofing box. After proofing, this is the fully active culture.

3. Punch down. Mix together the remaining ½ cup water, salt, sugar, and butter. Add to the dough and mix well. Reserve 1 cup of the flour for flouring the board. Mix and spoon knead the remaining 1¾ cups flour into the dough 1 cup at a time. When too stiff to mix by hand, transfer to the floured board and knead in the remaining flour.

4. Divide the dough in half and form each half into a ball. Roll out each ball into a rectangle about 12 by 18 inches. Cut each rectangle in half lengthwise, then cut each half into 2 rectangles each 6 by 9 inches. Finally, cut these rectangles into triangles.

6. Brush the triangles with the eggs and sprinkle with the caraway seeds. Roll up the triangles from the long side and place on a baking sheet. Proof 1½ hours at room temperature or 30 to 60 minutes at 85°.

7. Bake in a preheated oven at 375° for 20 minutes. Cool on wire racks.

PIZZA

RECIPE WITH **LIQUID** CULTURE   Makes four 12- to 13-inch pizzas

It's not the topping that gives sourdough pizza an Old World flavor. It's the crust. The choice of topping is yours, but don't try this recipe unless you are prepared to become addicted.

> 2 cups cold liquid culture   1½ teaspoons salt
> 4¾ cups white flour   2 tablespoons vegetable oil
> 1 cup water   Cornmeal or semolina

1. Mix the liquid culture with 1 cup of the flour and ¼ cup water in a large mixing bowl. This is the working culture. Proof 12 hours at room temperature (68° to 72°) or 6 hours in a proofing box at 85°.

2. Add 1 cup of the flour and ¼ cup of the water. Mix and knead until smooth. Proof 8 hours at room temperature or 4 hours at 85° in the proofing box. After proofing, this is the fully active culture.

3. Punch down. Mix together the remaining ½ cup water, the salt, and the oil. Add to the dough and mix well. Reserve 1 cup of the flour for flouring the board. Mix and spoon knead the remaining 1¾ cups flour into the dough 1 cup at a time. When too stiff to mix by hand, transfer to the floured board and knead in any remaining flour.

4. Divide the dough into 4 equal portions and form each into a ball. Roll out each ball into a 12- to 13-inch round about ⅛ inch thick. Gently fold each round in half and transfer to a baker's peel or rimless thin baking sheet sprinkled with cornmeal or semolina. Unfold the rounds and pinch a rim about ½ inch high along the edge of each round. Proof 1½ hours at room temperature or about 45 minutes in the proofing box.

5. Preheat a baking stone and an oven to 475°.

6. Add toppings of choice to the dough rounds. Transfer the pizzas to the hot baking stone (see Note).

7. Bake for 20 to 25 minutes, or until the edges of the crusts are brown. Remove from the oven with the baker's peel or baking sheet.

≈ *Note:* It takes practice to transfer the pizzas to the baking stone. As an alternative, proof and bake the pizza on a traditional pizza pan sprinkled with cornmeal, or, for a better crust, place the pizza pan on a hot baking stone. Cornmeal on the stone is not necessary for this method.

SALTED PRETZELS

RECIPE WITH **LIQUID** CULTURE   Makes 15 to 20 pretzels

Sourdough makes these basic partners for beer and spicy mustard a special treat.

2 cups cold liquid culture	*1 tablespoon sugar*
4¾ cups flour	*2 tablespoons oil*
1 cup water	*¼ cup baking soda*
1½ teaspoons salt	*Coarse salt*

1. Mix the liquid culture with 1 cup of flour in a large mixing bowl. This is the working culture. Proof 12 hours at room temperature (68° to 72°) or 6 hours in a proofing box at 85°.

2. Add 1 cup of the flour and ½ cup of the water. Mix and knead until smooth. Proof 8 hours at room temperature or 4 hours in the proofing box. After proofing, this is the fully active culture.

3. Punch down. Mix together the remaining ½ cup water, the salt, sugar, and oil. Add to the dough and mix well. Reserve 1 cup of the flour for flouring the board. Mix and spoon knead the remaining 1¾ cups flour into the dough 1 cup at a time. When too stiff to mix by hand, transfer to the floured board and knead in the remaining flour.

4. Divide the dough into 15 to 20 egg-sized balls. Roll each ball into a rope 14 inches long.

5. Twist and loop each rope into a pretzel shape. Proof for 2 hours at room temperature or 1 hour in the proofing box.

6. Bring a large saucepan filled with water to a boil and stir in the baking soda. Carefully drop the pretzels, one at a time, into the boiling water. Simmer briefly, turning once. Remove with a slotted spoon and place on cloth or paper towels until the water drains off.

7. Transfer the drained pretzels to a baking sheet. Make several oblique slashes in the crust of each pretzel with a sharp edge. Sprinkle with coarse salt.

8. Bake in a preheated oven at 425° for 30 to 40 minutes, or until browned.

BRAIDED EGG BREAD

RECIPE WITH **LIQUID** CULTURE   Makes 2 loaves

I enjoy making braided bread, and the finished product is attractive. I start the braid at one end and work to the other end. However, you may find it easier to start in the middle and braid in both directions, as described in the following note.

2 cups cold liquid culture	*1½ teaspoons salt*
6 cups flour	*2 tablespoons sugar*
½ cup water	*2 eggs, beaten*
1 cup milk	*2 tablespoons butter, melted*

Glaze

1 egg, beaten
Sesame seeds

1. Mix the liquid culture with 1 cup of the flour and ¼ cup of the water in a large mixing bowl. This is the working culture. Proof 12 hours at room temperature (68° to 72°) or 6 hours in a proofing box at 85°.

2. Add 1 cup of the flour and the remaining ¼ cup water. Mix and knead until smooth. Proof 8 hours at room temperature or 4 hours in the proofing box. After proofing, this is the fully active culture.

3. Punch down. Mix together the milk, salt, sugar, 2 eggs, and butter. Add to the dough and mix well. Reserve 1 cup of the flour for flouring the board. Mix and spoon knead the remaining 3 cups flour into the dough 1 cup at a time. When too stiff to mix by hand, transfer to the floured board and knead in the remaining flour.

4. Divide the dough in half and form each half into a ball. Divide each ball into 3 equal portions. Roll each portion into a rope about 18 inches long and ½ inch in diameter. Using 3 ropes for each loaf, braid the ropes. Place the braids on 2 baking sheets and proof 2 to 3 hours at room temperature or 1 to 2 hours in the proofing box.

5. To glaze the braids, brush the tops with beaten egg and sprinkle with sesame seeds. Bake in a preheated oven at 375° for 35 to 40 minutes. Remove from baking sheet and cool on wire racks.

≈ *Braiding Dough:* This is an alternative method for making strands of dough for braiding. First, form one ball into a log 3 inches in diameter. Then roll out the dough lengthwise into a rectangle 9 by 18 inches and ½ inch thick. Using a pizza cutter, cut 6 lengthwise strips each 1½ inches wide. Fold each strip in half lengthwise to make a rounder strip, and crimp the edges together. Using 3 strips for each braid, lay 1 strand on a work surface. Place the other 2 strands over it, so that they cross in the middle. Starting at the center and working toward one end, alternatively cross the outside strands over the one in the center. As you work, gently pull to taper the ends. When you reach the end, rotate the whole piece 180 degrees and braid to the other end. Pinch the strands together at each end and tuck them under the braid to finish.

ENGLISH MUFFINS

RECIPE WITH **SPONGE** CULTURE   Makes 20 muffins

Last winter while a storm raged outside and snow swirled past the windows, someone said, "I forgot to take anything out of the freezer for dinner." After several unacceptable suggestions, someone else remembered a dish we had forgotten for years, eggs Benedict. That idea was quickly rejected because we didn't have any English muffins, but it started us thinking. The next night we had eggs Benedict, and here's how we made our first sourdough English muffins.

½ cup cold sponge culture	2 teaspoons salt
6½ cups white flour	3 tablespoons butter, melted
1¼ cups water	White cornmeal
1 cup milk	

1. Mix the sponge culture with 1½ cups of the flour and 1 cup of the water in a large mixing bowl. This is the working culture. Proof 12 hours at room temperature (68° to 72°) or 6 hours in a proofing box at 85°.

2. Add 1 cup of the flour and the remaining ¼ cup of the water. Mix and knead until smooth. Proof 12 hours at room temperature or 6 hours in the proofing box. After proofing, this is the fully active culture.

3. Punch down. Mix together the milk, salt, and butter. Add to the dough and mix well. Reserve 1 cup of the flour for flouring the board. Mix and spoon knead the remaining 3 cups flour into the dough 1 cup at a time. When too stiff to mix by hand, transfer to the floured board and knead in the remaining flour.

4. Divide the dough in half and form each half into a ball. Roll out each ball into a flat oval about ½ inch thick. With a 4-inch biscuit or cookie cutter, cut out 20 muffins. (You can instead remove the lid from an empty 15-ounce can or a water glass of the same diameter.)

5.   Lightly grease 2 baking sheets and dust with white cornmeal. Place the muffins on the prepared sheets and proof 3 hours at room temperature or 2 hours in the proofing box.

6.   Cook on a large electric griddle preheated to 400°. After 2 minutes, when the bottoms are browned, reduce the heat to 325°, turn the muffins, and cook 8 minutes on the other side. Then turn again and cook another 6 minutes, or alternatively, bake in a preheated oven at 450° for 7½ minutes. Turn them over and bake an additional 7½ minutes. Transfer to wire racks to cool.

≈   *Eggs Benedict:* I know this is a sourdough book, but you really must know the final steps to appreciate English muffins: eggs Benedict. The essential ingredients in addition to those marvelous muffins include a slice of ham, a poached egg or two, and hollandaise sauce. There are great recipes for the sauce in *Joy of Cooking,* but you can also buy a packet of dry mix that is quick, easy, and a reasonable substitute. You split the muffins, add a slice of ham, top that with a poached egg, and finish with the hollandaise. In addition, I top mine with asparagus spears, but there are infinite variations. Over the years I have had lots of eggs Benedict, but they've never compared to those made with my own sourdough English muffins. Warning: You try this one at your own risk. They're addictive!

WHOLE-WHEAT MUFFINS

RECIPE WITH **LIQUID** CULTURE   Makes 12 to 14 muffins

These hearty muffins will probably work best with a fast culture, such as our Russian culture. I have, however, used our Original San Francisco culture with success.

2 cups whole-wheat flour	*1 teaspoon salt*
2 cups all-purpose white flour	*2 tablespoons sugar*
2 cups cold liquid culture	*3 tablespoons butter, melted*
½ cup water	*1 egg, beaten*
1 cup milk	

1. Combine the flours and mix well. To make the working culture, mix the liquid culture with 1 cup of the flour mixture and ¼ cup of the water in a large mixing bowl. Proof 12 hours at room temperature (68° to 72°) or 6 hours in a proofing box at 85°.

2. Add 1 cup of the flour mixture and the remaining ¼ cup water. Mix and knead until smooth. Proof 8 hours at room temperature or 4 hours at 85° in the proofing box. After proofing, this is the fully active culture.

3. Punch down. Mix together the milk, salt, sugar, butter, and egg. Add to the dough and mix well. Mix the remaining 2 cups flour into the batter-dough. Spoon the batter into muffin tins or drop by spoonfuls onto a baking sheet.

4. Bake in a preheated oven at 400° for 20 to 25 minutes, or until browned. Remove the muffins from the pans and cool on wire racks.

BUTTERFLAKE ROLLS

RECIPE WITH **LIQUID** CULTURE   Makes 8 to 10 rolls

This is a fun, buttery treat with delicious sourdough flavor.

2 cups cold liquid culture
4 cups all-purpose flour
½ cup water
½ cup milk

1 teaspoon salt
1 tablespoon sugar
¾ cup butter, melted
1 egg, beaten

Glaze

1 egg, beaten
Sesame seeds

1. Mix the liquid culture with 1 cup of the flour and ¼ cup of the water in a large mixing bowl. This is the working culture. Proof 12 hours at room temperature (68° to 72°) or 6 hours in a proofing box at 85°.

2. Add 1 cup of the flour and the remaining ¼ cup water. Mix and knead until smooth. Proof 8 hours at room temperature or 4 hours in the proofing box. After proofing, this is the fully active culture.

3. Punch down. Mix together the milk, salt, sugar, ¼ cup of the butter, and the egg. Add to the dough and mix well. Reserve 1 cup of the flour for flouring the board. Mix and spoon knead the remaining 1 cup flour into the dough. Transfer to the floured board and knead in the remaining flour.

4. Divide the dough into 8 to 10 equal balls. Dust each ball lightly with flour and flatten to a thin oval approximately 18 inches in diameter by hand or with a rolling pin.

5. Brush each oval with some of the remaining ½ cup melted butter and, starting from a long side, roll into a tight rope. Roll the ropes back and forth on the board until they double in length. Coil each rope into a round, then flatten gently with your hand or rolling pin into an 8-inch

round. Place on a baking sheet and proof 1 hour at room temperature or 2 hours in the proofing box.

6.   Brush with beaten egg and sprinkle with sesame seeds. Bake in a preheated oven at 400° for 12 to 15 minutes, or until browned. Remove the rolls from the baking sheet and cool on a wire rack.

DINNER ROLLS

RECIPE WITH **LIQUID** CULTURE   Makes 8 to 20 rolls

This recipe makes 8 to 12 Parker House rolls or 16 to 20 dinner rolls. I use all-purpose flour for a lighter texture. The rolls can be glazed with poppyseeds or sesame seeds if you like. Just before baking, brush the tops with beaten egg and sprinkle with the seeds.

2 cups cold liquid culture	*1 teaspoon salt*
4 cups all-purpose flour	*1 tablespoon sugar*
½ cup water	*3 tablespoons butter, melted*
½ cup milk	*1 egg, beaten*

1. Mix the liquid culture with 1 cup of the flour and ¼ cup of the water in a large mixing bowl. This is the working culture. Proof 12 hours at room temperature (68° to 72°) or 6 hours in a proofing box at 85°.

2. Add 1 cup of the flour and the remaining ¼ cup of water. Mix and knead until smooth. Proof 8 hours at room temperature or 4 hours in the proofing box. After proofing, this is the fully active culture.

3. Punch down. Mix together the milk, salt, sugar, 2 tablespoons of the butter, and the egg. Add to the dough and mix well. Reserve 1 cup of the flour for flouring the board. Mix and spoon knead the remaining 1 cup into the dough. Transfer to the floured board and knead in the remaining flour.

4. For Parker House rolls, roll out the dough ½ inch thick. With a 3-inch cookie cutter or biscuit cutter, cut out 8 to 12 rounds. (You can instead remove the lid of an empty can 3 inches in diameter or a water glass the same diameter.) Using a table knife, make a crease in each round slightly off the center. Brush the rounds lightly with the remaining 1 tablespoon butter. Using the crease as a guide, fold the larger part over the smaller of each round. Place on a baking sheet and proof at room temperature 2 hours or in the proofing box 1 hour.

5. For dinner rolls, divide the dough into 16 to 20 small balls. Place them side by side in an 8-inch square baking pan. Proof as for Parker House rolls until they rise above the sides of the pan.

6. Bake in a preheated oven at 375° for 20 to 25 minutes, or until browned. Remove the rolls from the pan and cool on wire racks or serve hot.

POPPYSEED ROLLS

RECIPE WITH **LIQUID** CULTURE   Makes 12 to 15 rolls

When I end up with extra dough from almost anything, I'll makes these rolls.

2 cups cold liquid culture	*1 teaspoon salt*
4 cups all-purpose flour	*1 tablespoon sugar*
½ cup water	*2 tablespoons butter, melted*
½ cup milk	*1 egg, beaten*

Glaze

1 egg, beaten
2 tablespoons milk
Poppyseeds

1. Mix the liquid culture with 1 cup of the flour and ¼ cup of the water to the culture in a large mixing bowl. This is the working culture. Proof 12 hours at room temperature (68° to 72°) or 6 hours in a proofing box at 85°.

2. Add 1 cup of the flour and the remaining ¼ cup water. Mix and knead until smooth. Proof 8 hours at room temperature or 4 hours in the proofing box. After proofing, this is the fully active culture.

3. Punch down. Mix together the milk, salt, sugar, butter, and egg. Add to the dough and mix well. Reserve 1 cup of the flour for flouring the board. Mix and spoon knead the remaining 1 cup flour into the dough. Transfer to the floured board and knead in the remaining flour.

4. Divide the dough into 12 to 15 equal balls. Flatten each ball into an oval about ½ inch thick and place on a baking sheet.

5. To make the glaze, combine the egg and milk and brush the mixture on the rolls. Sprinkle with poppyseeds. Make a slash in the top of each roll. Proof 2 hours at room temperature or 1 to 2 hours in the proofing box.

6. Bake in a preheated oven at 425° for 20 to 25 minutes. Remove from the baking sheet and cool on wire racks.

HAMBURGER BUNS

RECIPE WITH **LIQUID** CULTURE   Makes 8 buns

You won't find these buns at the fast-food chains. Burgers served on them are truly sublime.

2 cups cold liquid culture	*1 teaspoon salt*
4¾ cups flour	*Sesame seeds*
1¼ cups water	

1. Mix the liquid culture with 1 cup of the flour and ¼ cup of the water in a large mixing bowl. This is working culture. Proof 12 hours at room temperature (68° to 72°) or 6 hours in a proofing box at 85°.

2. Add 1 cup of the flour and ½ cup of the water. Mix and knead until smooth. Proof 8 hours at room temperature or 4 hours in the proofing box. After proofing, this is the fully active culture.

3. Punch down. Dissolve the salt in the remaining ½ cup water. Add to the dough and mix well. Reserve 1 cup of the flour for flouring the board. Mix and spoon knead the remaining 1¾ cups flour into the dough 1 cup at a time. When too stiff to mix by hand, transfer to the floured board and knead in the remaining flour.

4. Roll out the dough ½ inch thick. With a 4-inch cookie cutter or biscuit cutter, cut out rounds. (You can instead use an empty 15-ounce can with the lid removed or a water glass of the same diameter.) Place on a baking sheet, sprinkle with the sesame seeds, and proof at room temperature 3 to 4 hours or in the proofing box 2 to 3 hours.

5. Bake in a preheated oven at 350° for 15 to 18 minutes. Remove from the baking sheet and cool on wire racks.

BREADS OF
THE MIDDLE EAST

Our sourdough culture from Saudi Arabia will produce distinctive flavors in any leavened bread, though when we discovered it, we found it being used for flatbreads. My favorite is Khubz Arabi (following), the pita of the desert. The culture from Bahrain and two more from Egypt represent a versatile collection of Middle Eastern culture that no book on traditional sourdoughs can ignore. In the search for authentic sourdoughs, we were challenged to find and gain entrance to ethnic bakeries in areas where the culture had been handed down for generations. This was 1983 and some remote corners of the world had not yet been contaminated by commercial yeast. Now they have, and the cultures we collected then are no longer available today. Try these breads and taste the desert as it still is.

KHUBZ ARABI (ARAB BREAD)

RECIPE WITH **LIQUID** CULTURE   Makes 8 pitas

This hollow flatbread is probably the most exciting and delicious pita I have ever encountered. The soft, flat, white round with a pouch inside is produced throughout the Middle East, both commercially and in the home. For sentimental reasons, I guess, I use our culture from Saudi Arabia to make the recipe. It is great fun to watch the pita rounds start to form small surface blebs that suddenly expand to form the central cavity.

2 cups cold liquid culture
4¾ cups flour
1 cup water
1½ teaspoons salt

1 tablespoon sugar
1 tablespoon oil
Cornmeal or semolina

1. Mix the liquid culture with 1 cup of the flour and ¼ cup of the water in a large mixing bowl. This is the working culture. Proof 12 hours at room temperature (68° to 72°) or 6 hours in a proofing box at 85°.

2. Add 1 cup of the flour and ¼ cup of the water. Mix and knead until smooth. Proof 8 hours at room temperature or 4 hours in the proofing box. After proofing, this is the fully active culture.

3. Punch down. Mix together the remaining ½ cup water, salt, sugar, and oil. Add to the dough and mix well. Reserve 1 cup of the flour for flouring the board. Mix and spoon knead the remaining 1¾ cups flour into the dough 1 cup at a time. When too stiff to mix by hand, transfer to the floured board and knead in the remaining flour.

4. Divide the dough into 8 equal balls. Roll out each ball into a round about ¼ inch thick. Form 2 stacks with the rounds, separating the rounds with waxed paper or paper towels. Proof the rounds 1½ hours at room temperature or 30 minutes in the proofing box.

5. Preheat an oven and a baking stone to 500°. Sprinkle the hot stone with cornmeal or semolina just before transferring pitas. Using a baker's peel or a large spatula, slide the rounds onto the heated stone. Use care to

avoid damaging the surface of the rounds, or they may not puff completely. Bake for about 5 minutes, or until the rounds puff and start to brown. Remove from the oven with a peel or spatula and cool on wire racks.

≈   *Note:* If you use a baking sheet, the results are better if you place it on a preheated baking stone.

KHUBZ SAJ (THIN BREAD)

RECIPE WITH **LIQUID** CULTURE   Makes 25 to 30 flatbreads

This is the bread of the village Arab and Bedouin. It is still prepared in the campsites in a domed iron oven called a *saj,* that is placed over a fire of camel dung. In the ancient method, the thin rounds are draped over a special pillow with a hand grip on the back. When the oven is very hot, the flat rounds are slapped onto the iron surface and then removed within a minute or two. You can substitute a hot baking stone or metal baking sheet.

> *2 cups cold liquid culture*   *2 teaspoons salt*
> *4¾ cups flour*   *1 tablespoon sugar*
> *1 cup water*

1. Mix the liquid culture with 1 cup of flour and ¼ cup of the water in a large mixing bowl. This is the working culture. Proof 12 hours at room temperature (68° to 72°) or 6 hours in a proofing box at 85°.

2. Add 1 cup of the flour and ¼ cup of the water. Mix and knead until smooth. Proof 8 hours at room temperature or 4 hours in the proofing box. After proofing, this is the fully active culture.

3. Punch down. Dissolve the salt and sugar in the remaining ½ cup water. Add to the dough and mix well. Reserve 1 cup of the flour for flouring the board. Mix and spoon knead the remaining 1¾ cups flour into the dough 1 cup at a time. When too stiff to mix by hand, transfer to the floured board and knead in the remaining flour.

4. Preheat an oven and a baking sheet or stone to 450°.

5. Form the dough into balls about 2 inches in diameter. Roll out each ball into a very thin round. Each round should be about 10 inches in diameter.

6. As each one is formed, use a baker's peel or large spatula to transfer it to the hot baking sheet. Bake for 3 minutes. Remove from the oven with the peel or spatula and cool on wire racks.

MAFROODA

This white flatbread must not be allowed to form a pouch. To prevent it, press with the tines of a fork during baking if it starts to puff.

2 cups cold liquid culture	*1½ teaspoons salt*
4¾ cups flour	*1 teaspoon sugar*
¾ cup water	*2 tablespoons vegetable oil*

1. Mix the liquid culture with 1 cup of the flour and ¼ cup of the water in a large mixing bowl. This is the working culture. Proof 12 hours at room temperature (68° to 72°) or 6 hours in a proofing box at 85°.

2. Add 1 cup of the flour and ¼ cup of the water. Mix and knead until smooth. Proof 8 hours at room temperature or 4 hours in the proofing box. After proofing, this is the fully active culture.

3. Punch down. Mix together the remaining ¼ cup water, the salt, sugar, and oil. Add to the dough and mix well. Reserve 1 cup of the flour for flouring the board. Mix and spoon knead the remaining 1¾ cups flour into the dough 1 cup at a time. When too stiff to mix by hand, transfer to the floured board and knead in the remaining flour.

4. Lightly brush a baking sheet with oil and preheat it in an oven to 500°.

5. Form the dough into 10 equal balls. Flatten each ball by hand or with a rolling pin into a 10-inch round about ½ inch thick.

6. As each round is formed, use a floured baker's peel or large spatula to transfer it to the preheated baking sheet or griddle. Bake 4 to 5 minutes. Turn and brown briefly on the second side. Press the breads with the tines of a fork if they start to puff.

≈ *Note:* The rounds can also be cooked in an electric frying pan on the highest setting with the lid on. Heat the pan until smoking hot before adding the rounds.

SALUF

RECIPE WITH **LIQUID** CULTURE   Makes 12 flatbreads

The flavor of this typical Arab bread comes from fermentation. As with many Arab breads, this one does not puff to form a pocket. To enjoy these breads as they are traditionally served, accompany with Hilbeh (following).

2¾ cups whole-wheat flour   *1 cup water*
2¾ cups white flour   *½ teaspoon salt*
2 cups cold liquid culture   *1 tablespoon oil*

1. Combine the flours and mix well. To make the working culture, mix the liquid culture with 1 cup of the flour mixture and ¼ cup of the water in a large mixing bowl. Proof 12 hours at room temperature (68° to 72°) or 6 hours in a proofing box at 85°.

2. Add 1 cup of the flour and ½ cup of the water. Mix and knead until smooth. Proof 8 hours at room temperature or 4 hours in the proofing box. After proofing, this is the fully active culture.

3. Punch down. Dissolve the salt in the remaining ¼ cup water. Add to the dough and mix well. Reserve 1 cup of flour mixture for flouring the board. Mix and spoon knead the remaining 2½ cups flour mixture into the dough 1 cup at a time. When too stiff to mix by hand, transfer to the floured board and knead in the remaining flour mixture.

4. Lightly brush a baking sheet with oil and preheat it in an oven to 550°.

5. Divide the dough into 12 equal balls. Using a rolling pin or your hand, flatten each ball into an oval about 6 inches in diameter and ½ inch thick. Prick the surface with a fork to prevent puffing during baking. Brush the tops of the flatbreads lightly with oil.

6. Using a lightly floured baker's peel or large spatula, transfer 2 rounds to the heated baking sheet. Bake for 4 to 5 minutes, or until tops are lightly browned. If the rounds start to puff, press lightly with a fork. Repeat with the remaining rounds. Serve warm.

≈   *Hilbeh:* In a bowl, soak 2 teaspoons fenugreek seeds in ½ cup water for 12 to 18 hours, or until a jelly-like coating has formed on the seeds. Drain. In a blender, combine the drained seeds, ¼ cup chopped fresh cilantro, ½ teaspoon salt, 2 teaspoons fresh lemon juice, and 1 small fresh hot chile (seeds removed, optional). Process, adding enough water to form a thick paste. Store covered in the refrigerator until serving.

BREADS OF
SOUTH AFRICA

I have never encountered a sourdough culture capable of satisfactorily leavening a 100 percent whole-wheat dough. For that matter I have never seen a sourdough culture *grown* in 100 percent whole wheat. Until now. There is such a sourdough. It came to me from Cape Town, South Africa. The wild yeast and lactobacilli of this culture are completely unknown to me or, so far as I know, anyone else. The organisms are certainly different from any that I have used previously. For a better description see page 195 in the section on Wild Cultures from Sourdoughs International.

I have now grown this culture in 100 percent whole-wheat flour and in 100 percent white flour and subsequently baked sourdough loaves with both cultures. I think the results were both challenging and exceptionally good. At press time, my experience with the culture was limited, but I have urged the publisher to include two recipes, one with the whole-wheat culture, one with the white flour culture, but both with the South African organisms. The possibilities of using these two cultures with various combinations of flour are exciting.

100 PERCENT WHOLE-WHEAT SOURDOUGH

RECIPE WITH **LIQUID** CULTURE   Makes two 1½ pound loaves

This recipe uses a culture grown entirely in whole wheat and with 100 percent whole-wheat flour as the major ingredient. As a result it is a very dry dough, and kneading may be somewhat difficult. You may find it necessary to add additional water, but this should be done cautiously or the dough may become too moist.

> 1 cup whole-wheat liquid culture
> 5 cups whole-wheat flour
>
> 1½ cups water
> 1½ teaspoons salt

1. Mix the liquid culture with 1 cup of the flour and ¼ cup of the water in a large mixing bowl. This is the working culture. Proof 12 hours at room temperature (68° to 72°) or 6 hours in a proofing box at 85°.

2. Add 1 cup of the flour and ½ cup of the water. Mix and knead until smooth. Proof 8 hours at room temperature or 4 hours in the proofing box. After proofing, this is the fully active culture.

3. Punch down. Dissolve the salt in the remaining ½ cup of water. Add to the dough and mix well. Reserve 1 cup of flour for flouring the board. Mix and spoon knead the remaining 2 cups flour into the dough 1 cup at a time. When too stiff to mix by hand, transfer to the floured board and knead in the remaining flour.

4. Form 2 pan loaves, and proof them at the same temperature used above until the dough rises about 1 inch above the pan tops (3 to 5 hours).

5. Bake in a preheated oven at 375° for 40 to 45 minutes. Remove from the pans and cool on wire racks.

SOUTH AFRICAN CULTURE IN A WHITE-FLOUR BASE

RECIPE WITH **LIQUID** CULTURE   Makes two 1½ pound loaves

This recipe uses a liquid culture containing whole-wheat organisms in a white-flour base.

1 cup liquid culture in a   *1½ cups water*
white flour base   *1½ teaspoons salt*
5½ cups white flour

1.   Mix the liquid culture with 1 cup of the flour and ½ cup of the water in a large mixing bowl. This is the working culture. Proof 12 hours at room temperature (68° to 72°) or 6 hours in a proofing box at 85°.

2.   Add 1 cup of flour and ½ cup of water. Mix and knead until smooth. Proof 8 hours at room temperature or 4 hours in the proofing box. After proofing, this is the fully active culture.

3.   Punch down. Dissolve the salt in the remaining ½ cup of water and mix with the dough. Reserve 1 cup of flour for flouring the board. Mix and spoon knead the remaining 2½ cups flour into the dough 1 cup at a time. When too stiff to mix by hand, transfer to the floured board and knead in the remaining flour.

4.   Form 2 pan loaves, and proof them at the same temperature used above until the dough rises about 1 inch above the pan tops (3 to 5 hours).

5.   Bake in a preheated oven at 375° for 40 to 45 minutes. Remove from the pans and cool on wire racks.

BATTER BREADS

Sourdough cultures are as successful with batter breads as they are with other breads. Batters are lighter doughs that are mixed entirely by beating, either by hand or with an electric mixer. No kneading is involved. I have included a basic recipe for sourdough batter that you can use with any culture. Each of the recipes in this section starts with this unbaked batter and then calls for adding special ingredients to create a variety of breads. Some ingredients add extra fluids to the recipes and you may need to add additional flour to maintain the consistency of the batter. When adding the ingredients, mix them into the culture before adding the flour for the best results. The basic recipe makes a good white batter bread when baked.

BASIC SOURDOUGH BATTER

RECIPE WITH **LIQUID** CULTURE   Makes about 5 cups batter

This is the sourdough batter called for as the first ingredient in all the batter bread recipes that follow.

2 cups cold liquid culture	2 tablespoons sugar
3-plus cups white flour	2 tablespoons butter, melted
½ cup cold water	½ cup milk
1 teaspoon salt	

1. Mix the liquid culture with 2 cups of the flour and the water. Proof 12 hours at room temperature (68° to 72°) or 6 hours in a proofing box at 85°.

2. Add the salt, sugar, and butter to the milk and mix. Add to the dough and mix well. Add the remaining 1 cup flour and mix vigorously. The yield is approximately 3½ cups of basic sourdough batter. If you wish to bake a white batter bread, proceed through steps 3 to 6 below.

3. Grease a 4½ x 8½-inch loaf pan if not nonstick. Spoon batter into the prepared pan.

4. Proof covered at 85° for 1 to 2 hours, or until dough rises ½ inch above the edge of the pan.

5. Preheat oven to 350°. Bake 45 minutes.

6. Remove loaf from pan and cool on a wire rack.

BANANA BATTER BREAD

Makes 2 loaves

In addition to being easy, this combination of sourdough, bananas, and nuts results in a pleasing and unusual texture.

Basic Sourdough Batter
(page 144)
1 egg, beaten

1 cup mashed banana
½ cup sugar
½ cup chopped nuts

1. Combine the sourdough batter, egg, banana, sugar, and nuts in a large mixing bowl and mix well.

2. Spoon the batter into two 8½ by 4½ by 2½-inch pans. Cover lightly with plastic wrap and proof 3 hours at room temperature or 1 to 2 hours in a proofing box at 85°, or until the dough rises ½ inch above the pan tops.

3. Bake in a preheated oven at 350° for 45 minutes. Remove from the pans and cool on wire racks.

CHEESE BATTER BREAD

Makes 2 loaves

Just a glance at the ingredients should convince you to try this recipe. The choice of cheese is yours.

Basic Sourdough Batter
  (page 144)
2 eggs, beaten

1 cup grated cheese
½ teaspoon garlic powder
2 teaspoons caraway seeds

1. Combine the sourdough batter, eggs, cheese, garlic powder, and caraway seeds in a large mixing bowl and mix well.

2. Spoon the batter into two 8½ by 4½ by 2½-inch pans. Cover lightly with plastic wrap and proof 3 hours at room temperature or 1 to 2 hours in a proofing box at 85°, or until the dough rises ½ inch above the pan tops.

3. Bake in a preheated oven at 350° for 45 minutes. Remove from the pans and cool on wire racks.

CORN BATTER BREAD

Makes 2 loaves

This is not your standard corn bread. The sage, celery seeds, and cornmeal give the sourdough base an earthy quality.

Basic Sourdough Batter
(page 144)
1 teaspoon ground sage

2 teaspoons celery seeds
½ cup yellow cornmeal

1. Combine the sourdough batter, sage, celery seeds, and cornmeal in a large mixing bowl and mix well.

2. Spoon the batter into two 8½ by 4½ by 2½-inch pans. Cover lightly with plastic wrap and proof 3 hours at room temperature or 1 to 2 hours in a proofing box at 85°, or until the dough rises ½ inch above the pan tops.

3. Bake in a preheated oven at 350° for 45 minutes. Remove from the pans and cool on a wire rack.

CRANBERRY-HUCKLEBERRY BATTER BREAD

Makes 2 loaves

Cranberries have become a popular ingredient in bakery goods. Paired with huckleberries, the combination is hard to beat. Here is a good chance to sample that combination in a sourdough.

Basic Sourdough Batter
(page 144)
½ cup sweetened dried
cranberries

½ cup frozen huckleberries
Flour

1. Combine sourdough batter, cranberries, and huckleberries in a large mixing bowl and mix well. Add more flour as needed for proper thickness of consistency.

2. Spoon the batter into two 8½ by 4½ by 2½-inch pans. Cover lightly with plastic wrap and proof 3 hours at room temperature or 1 to 2 hours in a proofing box at 85°, or until the dough rises ½ inch above the pan tops.

3. Bake in a preheated oven at 350° for 45 minutes. Remove from the pans and cool on wire racks.

DILL BATTER BREAD

Makes 2 loaves

This bread is great for informal gatherings like an evening of card games or for rainy-day snacking.

Basic Sourdough Batter
(page 144)
1 cup grated Parmesan cheese

½ cup chopped onion
2 teaspoons dill seeds

1. Combine the sourdough batter, cheese, onion, and dill seeds in a large mixing bowl and mix well.

2. Spoon the batter into two 8½ by 4½ by 2½-inch loaf pans. Cover lightly with plastic wrap and proof 3 hours at room temperature or 1 to 2 hours in a proofing box at 85°, or until the dough rises ½ inch above the pan tops.

3. Bake in a preheated oven at 350° for 45 minutes. Remove from the pans and cool on wire racks.

LIMPA BATTER BREAD

Makes 2 loaves

Sourdough limpas in any form are wonderful. Of all the batter breads, this is probably my favorite.

Basic Sourdough Batter
  (page 144)
2 tablespoons molasses
1 teaspoon caraway seeds

Grated zest of 1 orange
1 cup rye flour
¼ cup milk

1. Combine the sourdough batter, molasses, caraway seeds, orange zest, rye flour, and milk in a large mixing bowl and mix well.

2. Spoon the batter into two 8½ by 4½ by 2½-inch pans. Cover lightly with plastic wrap and proof 3 hours at room temperature or 1 to 2 hours in a proofing box at 85°, or until the dough rises ½ inch above pan tops.

3. Bake in a preheated oven at 350° for 45 minutes. Remove from the pans and cool on wire racks.

NUT-RAISIN BATTER BREAD

Makes 2 loaves

Here is an interesting breakfast bread with the flavor of cinnamon rolls.

Basic Sourdough Batter   *1 teaspoon ground nutmeg*
  (page 144)   *1 cup raisins*
1 teaspoon ground cinnamon   *½ cup chopped nuts*

1. Combine the sourdough batter, cinnamon, nutmeg, raisins, and nuts in a large mixing bowl and mix well.

2. Spoon the batter into two 8½ by 4½ by 2½-inch pans. Cover lightly with plastic wrap and proof 3 hours at room temperature or 1 to 2 hours in a proofing box at 85°, or until the dough rises ½ inch above the pan tops.

3. Bake in a preheated oven at 350° for 45 minutes. Remove from the pan and cool on wire racks.

WHOLE-WHEAT BATTER BREAD

Makes 2 loaves

This batter bread is heavier than most and may take a little longer to rise.

Basic Sourdough Batter
   (page 144)
1 cup whole-wheat flour

1 egg, beaten
3 tablespoons molasses

1. Combine the sourdough batter, flour, egg, and molasses in a large mixing bowl and mix well.

2. Spoon the batter into two 8½ by 4½ by 2½-inch pans. Cover lightly with plastic wrap and proof 3 hours at room temperature or 1 to 2 hours in a proofing box at 85°, or until the dough rises ½ inch above the pan tops.

3. Bake in a preheated oven at 350° for 45 minutes. Remove from the pans and cool on wire racks.

SOURDOUGH PANCAKES

Sourdough pancakes are fun and easy. The twelve-hour proof provides the flavor and leavening. Prospectors apparently never had enough time or couldn't plan that far ahead, so the genuine sourdough pancake was usually a thin and somewhat rubbery critter that required an appetite and affection, both of which the prospectors had. There are generations of their descendants who consume rubbery pancakes and extol their virtues. You have to try them for the experience, then form your own opinion.

If the "cakes" don't rise as much as desired, a little baking soda will do the job. If you decide to try it, dissolve it in warm water and add it to the batter just before cooking. Once added, the batter must be used immediately, or it will quickly go flat. Do not use more baking soda than the specified amount, or the sourdough flavor will be neutralized.

I think my pancake recipes allow enough time for sufficient rising. They are neither rubbery nor is the addition of the baking soda necessary. Serve them piping hot with syrups, fruits, or honey.

APPLESAUCE PANCAKES

RECIPE WITH **LIQUID** CULTURE   Makes 12 to 15 pancakes

Applesauce provides the flavor in this recipe. For a real treat, drop 2 apples, peeled, cored, and cut up, into your food processor. Chop almost to a purée, then substitute the purée for the applesauce.

2 cups cold liquid culture	*1 tablespoon sugar*
1 cup white flour	*½ cup smooth applesauce*
¼ cup water	*2 tablespoons butter, melted*
½ teaspoon salt	*1 egg, beaten*

1. Mix the liquid culture with the flour and water in a large mixing bowl. Cover lightly with plastic wrap and proof 12 hours at room temperature or 6 hours in a proofing box at 85°.

2. In a small bowl, mix together the salt, sugar, applesauce, butter, and egg. Just before cooking, gently fold the applesauce mixture into the culture and mix briefly.

3. Preheat a griddle to 400°.

4. With a pitcher or ladle, pour the batter onto the hot griddle, forming 2- to 3-inch rounds. Cook 2 to 4 minutes, or until bubbles form on surface. Turn and cook an additional 2 minutes. Serve hot.

≈ *Tip:* If the first pancakes you cook don't rise as much as desired, stir ½ teaspoon baking soda into the batter immediately before cooking.

AUSTRIAN RYE PANCAKES

RECIPE WITH **LIQUID** CULTURE   Makes 12 to 15 pancakes

There isn't a combination of rye and sourdough that isn't good. When you're searching for something special for Sunday morning breakfast, these pancakes are what you want.

½ cup white flour	½ teaspoon salt
½ cup rye flour	2 tablespoons sugar
2 cups cold liquid culture	2 tablespoons butter, melted
½ cup water	1 egg, beaten

1. Combine the flours and mix well. Mix the liquid culture with the flour mixture and ¼ cup of the water in a large mixing bowl. Cover lightly with plastic wrap and proof 12 hours at room temperature or 6 hours in a proofing box at 85°.

2. In a small bowl, mix together the salt, the remaining ¼ cup water, sugar, butter, and egg. Just before cooking, gently fold this mixture into the culture and mix briefly. If the batter is too thin, I add an extra tablespoon or more of white flour.

3. Preheat a griddle to 400°.

4. With a pitcher or ladle, pour the batter onto the hot griddle, forming 2- to 3-inch rounds. Cook 2 to 4 minutes, or until bubbles form on the surface. Turn and cook an additional 2 minutes, serve hot.

≈ *Tip:* If the first pancakes you cook don't rise as much as desired, stir ½ teaspoon baking soda into the batter immediately before cooking.

MAPLE PANCAKES

RECIPE WITH **LIQUID** CULTURE Makes 12 to 15 pancakes

There are artificial maple flavorings, but none are an adequate substitute for the real thing—especially in these pancakes.

2 cups cold liquid culture	2 tablespoons butter, melted
1 cup white flour	¼ cup pure maple syrup
¼ cup water	1 egg, beaten
½ teaspoon salt	

1. Mix the liquid culture with the flour and water in a large mixing bowl. Cover lightly with plastic wrap and proof 12 hours at room temperature or 6 hours at 85°.

2. In a small bowl, mix together the salt, butter, maple syrup, and egg. Just before cooking, gently fold this mixture into the culture and mix briefly.

3. Preheat a griddle to 400°.

4. With a pitcher or ladle, pour the batter onto the griddle, forming 2- to 3-inch rounds. Cook 2 to 4 minutes, or until bubbles form on the surface. Turn and cook an additional 2 minutes. Serve hot.

≈ *Tip:* If the first pancakes you cook don't rise as much as desired, stir ½ teaspoon baking soda into the batter immediately before cooking.

YUKON FLAPJACKS

RECIPE WITH **LIQUID** CULTURE   Makes 12 to 15 pancakes

Have the griddle piping hot before pouring on this batter. When a host of bubbles appears, it is time to turn the cakes. The Yukon culture adds charisma!

2 cups cold liquid culture   *2 tablespoons sugar*
1 cup white flour   *2 tablespoons oil*
½ cup water   *1 egg, beaten*
½ teaspoon salt

1. Mix the liquid culture with the flour and ¼ cup of the water in a large mixing bowl. Cover lightly with plastic wrap and proof 12 hours at room temperature or 6 hours in a proofing box at 85°.

2. In a small bowl, mix together the remaining ¼ cup water, salt, sugar, oil, and egg. Just before cooking, gently fold this mixture into the culture and mix briefly. If the batter is too thin, I add an extra tablespoon or more of flour.

3. Preheat a griddle to 400°.

4. With a pitcher or ladle, pour the batter onto the hot griddle, forming 2- to 3-inch rounds. Cook 2 to 4 minutes, or until bubbles form on the surface. Turn and cook for an additional 2 minutes. Serve hot.

≈   *Tip:* If the first pancakes you cook don't rise as much as desired, stir ½ teaspoon baking soda into the batter immediately before cooking.

SOURDOUGH WAFFLES

Sourdough waffles combine the unequaled flavor of the culture with the light texture of all good waffles. To achieve the latter, the eggs are separated and the whites are beaten to the soft peak stage. At the very last minute, just before baking, the whites are gently folded into the batter. Oil and preheat the waffle iron before pouring on the batter. Serve the waffles hot with syrups, fruits, or your favorite whipped toppings.

BLUEBERRY WAFFLES

RECIPE WITH LIQUID CULTURE   Makes three or four 8-inch waffles

Use fresh blueberries if possible, but frozen berries are a good second choice. If you live where you can pick wild huckleberries, like I do, you live in the right place.

2 cups cold liquid culture	*1 tablespoon sugar*
1 cup white flour, plus more as needed	*2 eggs, separated*
	1 cup blueberries
2 tablespoons butter, melted	*1 teaspoon salt*

1. Mix the liquid culture with the 1 cup flour in a large mixing bowl. Cover lightly with plastic wrap and proof 12 hours at room temperature or 6 hours in a proofing box at 85°.

2. Add the butter, sugar, egg yolks, berries, and salt with additional flour as needed for the desired consistency. If you like your waffles somewhat thick, as I do, it may require an extra cup.

3. Preheat a waffle iron.

4. Beat the egg whites until they form soft peaks. Gently fold into the batter.

5. Pour the batter onto the hot waffle iron and cook for 7 to 8 minutes, or according to the manufacturer's instructions. Repeat with the remaining batter. Serve hot.

BUTTERMILK WAFFLES

RECIPE WITH **LIQUID** CULTURE   Makes three or four 8-inch waffles

The buttermilk sold in stores today is usually made from pasteurized milk to which a culture has been added to improve the flavor and consistency. For a real treat, search out a country dairy for old-fashioned buttermilk, which is a residue of butter churning.

2 cups cold liquid culture	*2 tablespoons butter, melted*
1 cup white flour, plus more as needed	*1 tablespoon sugar*
½ cup buttermilk	*2 eggs, separated*
	1 teaspoon salt

1. Mix the liquid culture with the 1 cup flour in a large mixing bowl. Cover lightly with plastic wrap and proof 12 hours at room temperature or 6 hours in a proofing box at 85°.

2. Add the buttermilk, butter, sugar, egg yolks, and salt with additional flour as needed for the desired consistency. If you like your waffles somewhat thick, as I do, it may require an extra cup.

3. Preheat a waffle iron.

4. Beat the egg whites until they form soft peaks. Gently fold into the batter.

5. Pour the batter onto the hot waffle iron and cook for 7 to 8 minutes, or according to the manufacturer's instructions. Repeat with the remaining batter. Serve hot.

GINGERBREAD WAFFLES

RECIPE WITH **LIQUID** CULTURE   Makes three or four 8-inch waffles

The flavor of ginger is unique in either bread or waffles. Unless you've tried both, you have missed a treat.

2 cups cold liquid culture
1 cup white flour, plus more
    as needed
½ cup milk
2 tablespoons butter, melted
2 tablespoons firmly packed
    brown sugar

2 tablespoons molasses
2 eggs, separated
1 teaspoon ground ginger
1 teaspoon salt

1. Mix the liquid culture with the 1 cup flour in a large mixing bowl. Cover lightly with plastic wrap and proof 12 hours at room temperature or 6 hours in a proofing box at 85°.

2. Add the milk, butter, brown sugar, molasses, egg yolks, ginger, and salt with additional flour as needed for the desired consistency. If you like your waffles somewhat thick, as I do, it may require an extra cup.

3. Preheat a waffle iron.

4. Beat the egg whites until they form soft peaks. Gently fold into the batter.

5. Pour the batter onto the hot waffle iron and cook for 7 to 8 minutes, or according to the manufacturer's instructions. Repeat with the remaining batter. Serve hot.

HAM WAFFLES

RECIPE WITH **LIQUID** CULTURE   Makes three or four 8-inch waffles

Ham is another of those savory ingredients that's a perfect partner for sour-dough.

2 cups cold liquid culture	*2 tablespoons butter, melted*
1 cup white flour, plus more as needed	*1 tablespoon sugar*
½ cup milk	*2 eggs, separated*
	1 cup chopped ham

1. Mix the liquid culture with the 1 cup flour in a large mixing bowl. Cover lightly with plastic wrap and proof 12 hours at room temperature or 6 hours in a proofing box at 85°.

2. Add the milk, butter, sugar, egg yolks, and ham with additional flour as needed for the desired consistency. If you like your waffles somewhat thick, as I do, it may require an extra cup.

3. Preheat a waffle iron.

4. Beat the egg whites until they form soft peaks. Gently fold into the batter.

5. Pour the batter onto the hot waffle iron and cook for 7 to 8 minutes, or according to the manufacturer's instructions. Repeat with the remaining batter. Serve hot.

RYE WAFFLES

RECIPE WITH **LIQUID** CULTURE Makes three or four 8-inch waffles

It's hard to say whether rye waffles are better than rye pancakes unless you've tried both. Twice!

1 cup white flour, plus more as needed
½ cup rye flour
2 cups cold liquid culture
½ cup milk

2 tablespoons oil
1 tablespoon sugar
2 eggs, separated
1 teaspoon salt

1. Combine the 1 cup white flour and the rye flour and mix well. Mix the liquid culture with the flour mixture in a large mixing bowl. Cover lightly with plastic wrap and proof 12 hours at room temperature or 6 hours in a proofing box at 85°.

2. Add the milk, oil, sugar, egg yolks, and salt with additional white flour as needed for the desired consistency. If you like your waffles somewhat thick, as I do, it may require an extra cup.

3. Preheat a waffle iron.

4. Beat the egg whites until they form soft peaks. Gently fold into the batter.

5. Pour the batter onto the hot waffle iron and cook for 7 to 8 minutes, or according to the manufacturer's instructions. Repeat with the remaining batter. Serve hot.

SOUR CREAM WAFFLES

Does sour cream make sourdough more sour? Yes, but just a tad enhances the tang of sourdough.

2 cups cold liquid culture	*2 tablespoons butter, melted*
1 cup white flour, plus more as needed	*1 tablespoon sugar*
	2 eggs, separated
1 cup sour cream	*1 teaspoon salt*

1. Mix the liquid culture with the 1 cup flour in a large mixing bowl. Cover lightly with plastic wrap and proof 12 hours at room temperature or 6 hours in a proofing box at 85°.

2. Add the sour cream, butter, sugar, egg yolks, and salt with additional flour as needed for the desired consistency. If you like your waffles somewhat thick, as I do, it may require an extra cup.

3. Preheat a waffle iron.

4. Beat the egg whites until they form soft peaks. Gently fold into the batter.

5. Pour the batter onto the hot waffle iron and cook for 7 to 8 minutes, or according to the manufacturer's instructions. Repeat with the remaining batter. Serve hot.

WHOLE-WHEAT WAFFLES

RECIPE WITH **LIQUID** CULTURE   Makes three or four 8-inch waffles

You may need 1 extra cup of white flour to get the ideal waffle texture.

2 cups cold liquid culture
½ cup whole-wheat flour
1 cup white flour, plus more
*   as needed*
½ cup milk

2 tablespoons butter, melted
1 tablespoon sugar
2 eggs, separated
1 teaspoon salt

1. In a large mixing bowl, combine the liquid culture and flours. Mix until smooth. Cover lightly with plastic wrap and proof 12 hours at room temperature or 6 hours in a proofing box at 85°.

2. Add the milk, butter, sugar, egg yolks, and salt with additional flour as needed for the desired consistency. If you like your waffles somewhat thick, as I do, it may require an extra cup.

3. Preheat a waffle iron.

4. Beat the egg whites until they form soft peaks. Gently fold into the batter.

5. Pour the batter onto the hot waffle iron and cook for 7 to 8 minutes, or according to the manufacturer's instructions. Repeat with the remaining batter. Serve hot.

YUKON WAFFLES

RECIPE WITH **LIQUID** CULTURE   Makes three or four 8-inch waffles

These waffles will be lighter and better if you can proof the batter for an hour at room temperature just before adding the egg whites. Our Yukon culture has gone toward making a lot of these.

2 cups cold liquid culture	*2 tablespoons butter, melted*
1 cup white flour, plus more as needed	*2 tablespoons sugar*
	2 eggs, separated
¼ cup milk	*1 teaspoon salt*

1. Mix the liquid culture with the 1 cup flour in a large mixing bowl. Cover lightly with plastic wrap and proof 12 hours at room temperature or 6 hours in a proofing box at 85°.

2. Add the milk, butter, sugar, egg yolks, and salt with additional flour as needed for the desired consistency. If you like your waffles somewhat thick, as I do, it may require an extra cup.

3. Preheat a waffle iron.

4. Beat the egg whites until they form soft peaks. Gently fold into the batter.

5. Pour the batter onto the hot waffle iron and cook for 7 to 8 minutes, or according to the manufacturer's instructions. Repeat with the remaining batter. Serve hot.

BAKING SOURDOUGHS

Chapter 5

IN BREAD MACHINES

For longer than I care to admit, I've been skeptical that home bread machines would ever produce an acceptable sourdough. Those days are gone forever, and I'm delighted to eat a big serving of humble pie. What changed my mind? After acquiring our Original San Francisco culture with the wild yeast *Candida humilis* and the lactobacilli, *L. sanfrancisco,* I was motivated to learn more about what those organisms can do in terms of flavor, texture, and leavening. In various experiments using manual methods, I was particularly impressed with the very long leavening power of the culture and the truly excellent flavor. Much to my surprise, the Original also performed extremely well at room temperature.

I felt challenged to determine just how our other nine cultures compared with the Original. It was with some trepidation that I set up a series of experiments to determine the leavening power of the cultures at room temperatures (68° to 72°) and at 85°. Since I had inherited two machines, the Breadman Dream and the Ultimate TR2200C, both with "bake only" cycles, it looked like an unusual opportunity to test each culture simultaneously at the two temperatures.

Each test went something like this: For the control I used the Original, combining ½ cup sponge culture, 2 cups white flour, and 1¼ cups of water in a pan from each machine. Next, I started the dough cycle on both machines and let them mix the contents for 15 minutes. Then I took both pans out of their machines and put one in a proofing box at 85° and the other on the counter at about 68°. They both proofed overnight (12 hours). The next morning, both cultures were quite similar and looked moderately active. At this point I returned the pans to their machines and added 2 cups flour and ⅓ cup water to each and then mixed them for 10 minutes. I again removed the pans from the machines and the leavening race started. In just 2 hours the 85° dough was above the pan top, and I punched it down with a spatula. The 68° dough reached the pan top just 30 minutes later. Both doughs were in a dead heat 2 hours later, and both were again punched down. On the third rise, the 68° dough was at the top again in 2 hours, and I returned it to the machine and started the bake only cycle. It demonstrated a modest "oven spring" that convinced me it was not overproofed. The 85° dough began to slow on the third rise and required 3 hours to reach the pan top. On baking it showed a slight dough retraction, indicating that it was somewhat overproofed.

In summary, the wild yeast in those doughs not only pushed them above the pan tops in two hours at both temperatures, but they repeated the performance twice more. More was to come, however. All nine of the "old" cultures did essentially the same thing. To be sure, some of them took a little longer to make the third rise, but two of them even went up for a fourth time. I have rarely been more surprised! To top it off, some fabulous sourdough textures were produced by these machines, and the flavor and sourness were both excellent. As mentioned, I've been dieting on humble pie.

Perhaps I shouldn't have been surprised at all. In retrospect, I think some analogies probably exist among home baking machines, Egyptian bread molds, La Cloche stoneware, and, yes, even masonry ovens. All of them, to some extent, represent closed systems that trap the moisture from baking doughs and favorably influence dough texture, much like steam-injected ovens. Some work more efficiently than others.

Baking sourdoughs in a bread machine is not as simple as making other types of bread in a machine. The fermentation by which lactobacilli produce the sourdough flavor still takes about twelve hours or more before a fully active culture is achieved whether the bread is made by hand or machine. The real problem with machine-made sourdoughs is getting the dough to adhere to the machine's schedule and vice versa. When the "last rise" cycle starts, the wild yeast must be at peak activity to leaven the loaf completely before baking starts. If not, the results will not please you at all. In the last five years, however, programming of some machines has improved, permitting the loaf to rise or ferment indefinitely until the baker decides it is time to turn on the bake cycle. So-called bake only cycles have dramatically changed the way sourdoughs can be produced in machines.

Ten years ago, I would have insisted the best proofing temperatures were between 85° to 95°. Now I know better, and I do a lot of my sourdoughs at room temperature (68° to 72°) because too many machines are hotter than I prefer. The solution to that, of course, is simple. I use the machine for mixing and kneading, then remove the pan and let the culture or dough ferment on the counter at room temperature. When the dough has fermented sufficiently to produce the flavor or sourness I like, or when it has leavened to the top, I put the pan back in the machine and start the bake only cycle. That's easy enough if your machine has that particular program. What do you do if it doesn't? That's simple, too. Preheat your conventional oven to 400°, and pop your machine pan into it. For machines with vertical pans, which are higher than horizontal ones, you may have to rearrange your oven racks a bit. In testing various machines that don't have the bake only cycle, I have done this little trick with my convection oven, and it works like a charm.

You can do the same thing with retarding (see page 43). When you run out of time at the end of the day, it is nice to slow down the fermentation process, or, as the term suggests, cool it. And that's exactly what I do. Remove the pan with its dough and stick it in your refrigerator. The temperature inside mine averages between 38° and 42°. At that level, the wild yeast and lactobacilli will continue to ferment but at a slower pace. I do the same thing occasionally with hand-formed pan loaves, and I'm always surprised to see how much more they have leavened while in the refrigerator. Retarding also appears, as you might suspect, to result in a somewhat more intense flavor and in better texture, that is, larger and more irregular spaces and holes.

Activating and Culture Preparation

Without question, these two steps are as essential to sourdoughs made in your machine as they are for a hand method. Review pages 39 to 44. Your first challenge is to produce a stock culture from the dried culture. Don't minimize this effort. Once you get a good stock culture, you can reactivate it whenever you desire and it will perform beautifully in your machine.

The Machine Process

Of course, you cannot dump all the ingredients in the machine, select a program, hit the start button, and walk away until the bell rings announcing "Sourdough!" But with some hands-on management, your machine will eliminate a lot of the work and turn out better sourdoughs than you (or I) ever expected.

I have successfully and consistently baked good sourdoughs with a variety of machines, but none of them is designed specifically for breads that allow the user to set the last rising cycle as long as desired. The delay cycles, which almost all machines have, require the baker to load the ingredients carefully with the yeast on top to prevent any activity until the delay ends, at which time the relatively short cycles begin. This obviously is not designed for sourdoughs. The machines I have evaluated include two of the Breadman family, the Dream Model TR3000 and the '98 Ultimate TR2200C. Both have bake only cycles that do permit the dough to ferment as long as you wish. Be sure the Ultimate is the TR2200C, since the '97 Ultimate doesn't have the bake only cycle. The Dream has a vertical pan, 5¼ by 5¼ inches, while the Ultimate has a horizontal pan, 7½ by 5 inches. I also tested three Toastmaster machines, the Bread Box Model 1148X, with a small 6½ by 5¼-inch horizontal pan, the Corner Bakery-Bread & Dessert Maker Model 1193N, with a vertical pan 5½ by 5½ inches, and a larger Bread Box, Model 1142, with a horizontal pan, 7½ by 5¼ inches. The Zojirushi Model BBCC-S15 has a vertical pan that measures 5¼ by 5¼ inches.

All six machines perform mixing and kneading well, and all would be satisfactory using the dough cycle for the short intervals needed to produce sourdoughs. The temperature in the three Toastmaster models, however, exceeded 100° (one was 108°) during basic white bread cycles (excluding baking temperatures), which would be damaging to sourdough organisms if the dough cycle were completed. Similarly, maximum temperature of the Dream was 89°, of the Ultimate was 95°, and the Zojirushi was 85°. Since the Dream and the Ultimate are the only machines among the six with bake only cycles, they are preferred for sourdoughs. As has been pointed out, even those two require special attention if room temperature operation is desired.

In addition to timing and temperature, correct dough consistency is critical for success with machine-mixed sourdoughs. This is a particular problem with sourdoughs because one is never precisely sure how much flour and water is added with the culture. If the dough is too thin, it will often rise well, then retract somewhat or collapse. If it is too thick, it may not rise as well. The problem is fairly easy to correct, providing you recognize it and add either a little additional water or flour, whichever is indicated.

The trick is to recognize the problem by watching the kneading paddle after the flour and ingredients have been added. After three or four minutes, when all the ingredients are well mixed, the dough should form a soft ball that catches and drags on the sides and bottom of the pan as the paddle revolves. If instead it forms a firm ball that revolves with or on the paddle and doesn't catch on the sides, it is too thick and isn't kneading properly. To correct this, add water, a tablespoon at a time, until the dough begins to adhere. If the dough doesn't form a ball, it is too thin and flour should be added a tablespoon at a time. Allow sufficient time after adding either flour or water for it to be incorporated into the dough before adding more. Most machines have two kneading cycles, and you should check the consistency on both.

Some machines, such as the Zojirushi, have a rod that projects from the side of the pan and catches the dough as it revolves. This provides a superior kneading action. Others have a paddle and pan shape that produces a peculiar formation in the dough that resembles a miniature tornado as it curls and twists up the sides of the pan. Judging paddle consistency takes experience with the machine you are using, since there is considerable variation in the size, shape, and ridges in the pan walls, all of which affect the efficiency of the kneading action.

The Dough Cycle

The bread machine has been promoted as the answer to simplified baking for the person with limited time who wants to program the machine to deliver fresh-baked bread at breakfast with only ten or fifteen minutes of effort. And it does a fair job of doing just that. Granted, the loaves will lack the appearance of an intriguing French loaf, with its slashed crust, and it will never turn out an Arab pita bread, a Swiss braid, a Russian round, or the pan of dinner rolls. But you can do all of that with the dough cycle, and it's easier than you think.

Once the dough cycle is complete, remove the dough from the machine with well-floured hands. Transfer it to the floured board and the fun begins. This dough is sometimes more moist than dough produced by hand, so don't hesitate to knead in a little additional flour if it appears too soft. Now you can shape the dough as you wish. Refer elsewhere in the book for instructions on forming and baking loaves, braids, pitas, or other choices.

Now, on to some new and interesting ways to make sourdoughs in machines. With a little more attention, that machine will do a fabulous job with sourdoughs.

Recipes

Each of the following recipes is designed to produce a two-pound loaf. For those who weigh things, the dough should weigh thirty-four to thirty-six ounces, since about two ounces of moisture will disappear during baking. You can even start with a cold culture right out of the refrigerator, since the machine, under your expert direction, will reactive the semidormant organisms before the final cycles start. The recipes are also crafted at a ratio of 63 percent flour to 37 percent water, a good machine consistency. In more complex recipes with multiple flours including ryes and bulgur or ingredients that absorb water in large amounts, more water will be required. Watch the paddle action to judge how much to add.

WORLD BREAD

RECIPE WITH **SPONGE** CULTURE   Makes one 2-pound loaf

This basic white bread is available around the world. It has probably been baked with all known sourdough cultures.

½ cup cold sponge culture	1 teaspoon salt
3¼ cups white flour	1 tablespoon sugar
1 cup water	1 tablespoon vegetable oil
¼ cup warm milk	

1. Place the sponge culture in the machine pan with 1 cup of the flour and ½ cup of the water. Machine mix and knead 15 minutes. Remove the pan from the machine, cover lightly with plastic wrap, and proof 12 hours at room temperature (68° to 72°) or 6 hours in a proofing box at 85°.

2. Return the pan to the machine and add 1 cup of the flour and the remaining ½ cup water. Mix 10 minutes. Remove the pan from the machine and proof 8 hours at room temperature or 4 hours in the proofing box.

3. Return the pan to the machine and add the warm milk, salt, sugar, oil, and the remaining 1¼ cups flour. Mix and knead 15 to 20 minutes.

4. Remove the pan from the machine and proof at the same temperature until the dough rises about ½ inch above the pan top (2 to 3 hours at room temperature; 1½ to 2 hours at 85°).

5. If the machine has a bake only cycle, return the pan to the machine and program the cycle to bake at 375° for 50 to 60 minutes. If not, move the pan to your preheated oven at 375° and bake for 45 minutes. Remove the loaf from the pan and cool on a wire rack.

ANISE RYE BREAD

RECIPE WITH **SPONGE** CULTURE   Makes one 2-pound loaf

Anise and rye blend surprisingly well in this unusual sourdough recipe.

1 cup rye flour	*1½ teaspoons salt*
3 cups white flour	*2 tablespoons vegetable oil*
½ cup cold sponge culture	*1 tablespoon sugar*
1½ cups water	*1 teaspoon ground aniseed*

1. Combine the flours and mix well. Place the sponge culture in the machine pan with 1 cup of the flour mixture and ½ cup of the water. Machine mix and knead 15 minutes. Remove the pan from the machine, cover lightly with plastic wrap, and proof 12 hours at room temperature (68° to 72°) or 6 hours in a proofing box at 85°.

2. Return the pan to the machine and add 1 cup of the flour mixture and ½ cup of the water. Mix for 10 minutes. Remove the pan from the machine, cover, and proof for 8 hours at room temperature or 4 hours in the proofing box.

3. Return the pan to the machine. Dissolve the salt in the remaining ½ cup water and add to the pan along with the oil, sugar, aniseed, and the remaining 2 cups flour mixture. Mix and knead 15 to 20 minutes.

4. Remove the pan from the machine and proof at the same temperature until the dough rises about ½ inch above the pan top (2 to 3 hours at room temperature; 1½ to 2 hours at 85°).

5. If the machine has a bake only cycle, return the pan to the machine and program the cycle to bake at 375° for 50 to 60 minutes. If not, move the pan to your preheated oven at 375° and bake for 45 minutes. Remove the loaf from the pan and cool on a wire rack.

CARAWAY RYE BREAD

RECIPE WITH **SPONGE** CULTURE   Makes one 2-pound loaf

Rye, caraway, and sourdough make a wonderful combination. This is a somewhat heavy dough and may do better with the addition of some gluten flour.

1 cup rye flour	*1½ cups water*
3 cups white flour	*1½ teaspoons salt*
½ cup cold sponge culture	*1 tablespoon caraway seeds*

1. Combine the flours and mix well. Place the sponge culture in the machine pan with 1 cup of the flour mixture and ½ cup of the water. Machine mix and knead 15 minutes. Remove the pan from the machine, cover lightly with plastic wrap, and proof 12 hours at room temperature (68° to 72°) or 6 hours in a proofing box at 85°.

2. Return the pan to the machine and add 1 cup of the flour mixture and ½ cup of water. Mix 10 minutes. Remove the pan from the machine and proof 8 hours at room temperature or 4 hours in the proofing box.

3. Return the pan to the machine. Dissolve the salt in the remaining ½ cup water and add to the pan along with the caraway seeds and remaining 2 cups flour mixture. Mix and knead 15 to 20 minutes.

4. Remove the pan from the machine and proof at the same temperature until the dough rises about ½ inch above the pan top (2 to 3 hours at room temperature; 1½ to 2 hours at 85°).

5. If your machine has a bake only cycle, return the pan to the machine and program the cycle to bake at 375° for 50 to 60 minutes. If not, move the pan to your preheated oven at 375° and bake for 45 minutes. Remove the loaf from the pan and cool on a wire rack.

OATMEAL BREAD

The rolled oats increase the fiber content of this white bread. I like old-fashioned rolled oats in this recipe, but you can substitute the quick-cooking types.

½ cup cold sponge culture	2 tablespoons firmly packed
4 cups white flour	brown sugar
1½ cups water	1½ cups rolled oats
1½ teaspoons salt	

1. Place the sponge culture in the machine pan with 1 cup of the flour and ½ cup of the water. Machine mix and knead for 15 minutes. Remove the pan from the machine, cover lightly with plastic wrap, and proof 12 hours at room temperature (68° to 72°) or 6 hours in a proofing box at 85°.

2. Return the pan to the machine and add 1 cup of the flour mixture and ½ cup of water. Mix 10 minutes. Remove the pan from the machine and proof 8 hours at room temperature or 4 hours in the proofing box.

3. Return the pan to the machine. Dissolve the salt in the remaining ½ cup water and add to the pan along with the brown sugar, rolled oats, and the remaining 2 cups flour. Mix and knead 15 to 20 minutes.

4. Remove the pan from the machine and proof at the same temperature until the dough rises about ½ inch above the pan top (2 to 3 hours at room temperature; 1½ to 2 hours at 85°).

5. If your machine has a bake only cycle, return the pan to the machine and program the cycle to bake at 375° for 50 to 60 minutes. If not, move the pan to your preheated oven at 375° and bake for 45 minutes. Remove the loaf from the pan and cool on a wire rack.

SAN FRANCISCO SOURDOUGH BREAD

RECIPE WITH **SPONGE** CULTURE   Makes one 2-pound loaf

This unquestionably is the best-known sourdough in the Western Hemisphere—if not in the world. On my list of bread-machine favorites, it remains number one! It seems incredible that this bread is produced by a wild culture using only flour, water, and salt. If you want a French loaf, use your dough cycle, form the loaf, and bake it in a conventional oven. The flavor really loses nothing in the pan loaf of a machine and the texture is incredible. The only culture I ever use for this recipe is our Original San Francisco.

½ cup cold sponge culture   *1¼ cups water*
4 cups white flour   *1 teaspoon salt*

1. Place the sponge culture in the machine pan with 1 cup of the flour and ½ cup of the water. Machine mix and knead 15 minutes. Remove the pan from the machine, cover lightly with plastic wrap, and proof 12 hours at room temperature (68° to 72°) or 6 hours in a proofing box at 85°.

2. Return the pan to the machine and add 1 cup of the flour and ½ cup of the water. Mix 10 minutes. Remove the pan from the machine and proof 8 hours at room temperature or 4 hours in the proofing box.

3. Return the pan to the machine. Dissolve the salt in the remaining ¼ cup water and add to the pan along with the remaining 2 cups flour mixture. Mix and knead 15 to 20 minutes.

4. Remove the pan from the machine and proof at the same temperature until the dough rises about ½ inch above the pan top (2 to 3 hours at room temperature; 1½ to 2 hours in the proofing box).

5. If your machine has a bake only cycle, return the pan to the machine and program the cycle to bake at 375° for 50 to 60 minutes. If not, move the pan to your preheated oven at 375° and bake for 45 minutes. Remove the loaf from the pan and cool on a wire rack.

SAUDI DATE BREAD

RECIPE WITH **SPONGE** CULTURE   Makes one 2¹/₂-pound loaf

I was concerned that the heavy load of dates and nuts in this recipe would weigh down the dough, but it rose beautifully. The loaf weighed 2½ pounds, which pushed the capacity of the machine. It was delectable!

½ cup cold sponge culture	2 tablespoons sugar
4 cups white flour	1 tablespoon olive oil
1½ cups water	1 cup chopped dates
1½ teaspoons salt	1 cup chopped walnuts

1. Place the sponge culture in the machine pan with 1 cup of the flour and ½ cup of the water. Machine mix and knead 15 minutes. Remove the pan from the machine, cover lightly with plastic wrap, and proof 12 hours at room temperature (68° to 72°) or 6 hours in a proofing box at 85°.

2. Return the pan to the machine and add 1 cup of the flour and ½ cup of the water. Mix 10 minutes. Remove the pan from the machine and proof 8 hours at room temperature or 4 hours in the proofing box.

3. Return the pan to the machine. Dissolve the salt in the remaining ½ cup water and add to the pan along with the sugar, oil, dates, walnuts, and the remaining 2 cups flour. Mix and knead 15 to 20 minutes.

4. Remove the pan from the machine and proof at the same temperature until the dough rises about ½ inch above the pan top (2 to 3 hours at room temperature; 1½ to 2 hours at 85°).

5. If your machine has a bake only cycle, return the pan to the machine and program the cycle to bake at 375° for 50 to 60 minutes. If not, move the pan to your preheated oven at 375° and bake for 45 minutes. Remove the loaf from the pan and cool on a wire rack.

SOUR CREAM RYE BREAD

RECIPE WITH **LIQUID** CULTURE   Makes one 2-pound loaf

This Austrian recipe is a great combination of flavors and is easy to make in any machine.

1 cup rye flour	*1 cup sour cream*
3 cups white flour	*2 tablespoons sugar*
½ cup cold liquid culture	*1 tablespoon vegetable oil*
1 cup water	*2 tablespoons caraway seeds*
1½ teaspoons salt	

1. Combine the flours and mix well. Place the liquid culture in the machine pan with 1 cup of the flour mixture and ½ cup of the water. Machine mix and knead 15 minutes. Remove the pan from the machine, cover lightly with plastic wrap, and proof 12 hours at room temperature (68° to 72°) or 6 hours in a proofing box at 85°.

2. Return the pan to the machine and add 1 cup of the flour and the remaining ½ cup water. Mix 10 minutes. Remove the pan from the machine and proof 8 hours at room temperature or 4 hours in the proofing box.

3. Return the pan to the machine. Dissolve the salt in the sour cream and add to the pan along with the sugar, oil, caraway seeds, and the remaining 2 cups flour mixture. Mix and knead 15 to 20 minutes.

4. Remove the pan from the machine and proof at the same temperature until the dough rises about ½ inch above the pan top (2 to 3 hours at room temperature; 1½ to 2 hours at 85°).

5. If your machine has a bake only cycle, return the pan to the machine and program the cycle to bake at 375° for 50 to 60 minutes. If not, move the pan to your preheated oven at 375° and bake for 45 minutes. Remove the loaf from the pan and cool on a wire rack.

SUNFLOWER BREAD

RECIPE WITH **LIQUID** CULTURE   Makes one 2-pound loaf

This recipe produces a light-textured, dark, nutty bread. Use raw sunflower seeds, not roasted, for best results.

> 1 cup whole-wheat flour
> 3 cups white flour
> ½ cup cold liquid culture
> 1 cup water
> 1½ teaspoons salt

> ½ cup milk
> 2 tablespoons sugar
> 2 tablespoons butter, melted
> 1 cup raw sunflower seeds

1. Combine the flours and mix well. Place the liquid culture in the machine pan with 1 cup of the flour mixture and ½ cup of the water. Machine mix and knead 15 minutes. Remove the pan from the machine, cover lightly with plastic wrap, and proof 12 hours at room temperature (68° to 72°) or 6 hours in a proofing box at 85°.

2. Return the pan to the machine and add 1 cup of the flour mixture and the remaining ½ cup water. Mix 10 minutes. Remove the pan from the machine and proof 8 hours at room temperature or 4 hours in the proofing box.

3. Return the pan to the machine. Dissolve the salt in the milk and add to the pan along with the sugar, butter, sunflower seeds, and the remaining 2 cups flour mixture. Mix and knead 15 to 20 minutes.

4. Remove the pan from machine and proof at the same temperature until the dough rises about ½ inch above the pan top (2 to 3 hours at room temperature; 1½ to 2 hours at 85°).

5. If your machine has a bake only cycle, return the pan to the machine and program the cycle to bake at 375° for 50 to 60 minutes. If not, move the pan to your preheated oven at 375° and bake for 45 minutes. Remove the loaf from the pan and cool on a wire rack.

SUNFLOWER SPELT BREAD

RECIPE WITH **LIQUID** CULTURE   Makes one 2-pound loaf

Purity Foods cautions that spelt gluten is much more fragile than other glutens. I doubt this is a significant problem with hand mixing, but in a machine it could be. In my test baking with spelt, I limited each machine knead to 10 minutes and kept an eye on the dough consistency. It rose very well.

2 cups spelt flour
2 cups white flour
½ cup cold liquid culture
1 cup water
1½ teaspoons salt

½ cup milk
2 tablespoons sugar
2 tablespoons butter, melted
1 cup raw sunflower seeds

1. Combine the flours and mix well. Place the liquid culture in the machine pan with 1 cup of the flour mixture and ½ cup of the water. Machine mix and knead 10 minutes. Remove the pan from the machine, cover lightly with plastic wrap, and proof 12 hours at room temperature (68° to 72°) or 6 hours in a proofing box at 85°.

2. Return the pan to the machine and add 1 cup of the flour mixture and the remaining ½ cup water. Mix 10 minutes. Remove the pan from the machine, cover, and proof 8 hours at room temperature or 4 hours at 85°.

3. Return the pan to the machine. Dissolve the salt in the milk and add to the pan along with the sugar, butter, sunflower seeds, and the remaining 2 cups flour mixture. Mix and knead 10 minutes.

4. Remove the pan from the machine and proof at the same temperature until the dough rises about ½ inch above the pan top (2 to 3 hours at room temperature; 1½ to 2 hours at 85°).

5. If your machine has a bake only cycle, return the pan to the machine and program the cycle to bake at 375° for 50 to 60 minutes. If not, move the pan to your preheated oven at 375° and bake for 45 minutes. Remove the loaf from the pan and cool on a wire rack.

LIGHT SWEDISH LIMPA

RECIPE WITH **SPONGE** CULTURE   Makes one 2-pound loaf

Limpas are rye breads with brown sugar or molasses. The orange zest should be coarsely grated. In my opinion, this is one of the best sourdough recipes.

1 cup rye flour	1 tablespoon vegetable oil
3 cups white flour	Grated zest from 1 orange
½ cup cold sponge culture	1 tablespoon caraway seeds
1½ cups water	1 tablespoon fennel seeds
1½ teaspoons salt	
2 tablespoons firmly packed brown sugar	

1. Combine the flours and mix well. Place the sponge culture in the machine pan with 1 cup of the flour mixture and ½ cup of the water. Machine mix and knead 15 minutes. Remove the pan from the machine, cover lightly with plastic wrap, and proof 12 hours at room temperature (68° to 72°) or 6 hours in a proofing box at 85°.

2. Return the pan to the machine and add 1 cup of the flour mixture and ½ cup of the water. Mix 10 minutes. Remove the pan from the machine and proof 8 hours at room temperature or 4 hours at 85°.

3. Return the pan to the machine. Dissolve the salt in the remaining ½ cup water and add to the pan along with the brown sugar, oil, zest, caraway seeds, fennel seeds, and the remaining 2 cups flour mixture. Mix and knead 15 to 20 minutes.

4. Remove the pan from the machine and proof at the same temperature until the dough rises about ½ inch above the pan top (2 to 3 hours at room temperature; 1½ to 2 hours at 85°).

5. If your machine has a bake only cycle, return the pan to the machine and program the cycle to bake at 375° for 50 to 60 minutes. If not, move the pan to your preheated oven at 375° and bake for 45 minutes. Remove the loaf from the pan and cool on a wire rack.

TANYA'S PEASANT BLACK BREAD

RECIPE WITH **LIQUID** CULTURE   Makes one 2-pound loaf

Every baker should try this recipe. The heavy dough requires a fast culture in the average machine cycle, but the options provided will improve the success rate in any machine. The heavy rye and wheat flours may suggest using a gluten flour, but try the recipe without it first. The coriander and molasses complement the sourdough flavor.

1 cup rye flour	*1½ teaspoons salt*
1 cup whole-wheat flour	*½ cup milk*
2 cups white flour	*1½ teaspoons ground*
½ cup cold liquid culture	*coriander*
1 cup water	*½ cup dark molasses*

1. Combine the flours and mix well. Place the liquid culture in the machine pan with 1 cup of the flour mixture and ½ cup of the water. Machine mix and knead 15 minutes. Remove the pan from the machine, cover lightly with plastic wrap, and proof 12 hours at room temperature (68° to 72°) or 6 hours in a proofing box at 85°.

2. Return the pan to the machine and add 1 cup of the flour mixture and the remaining ½ cup water. Mix 10 minutes. Remove the pan from the machine and proof 8 hours at room temperature or 4 hours at 85°.

3. Return the pan to the machine. Dissolve the salt in the milk and add to the pan along with the coriander, molasses, and the remaining 2 cups flour mixture. Mix and knead 15 to 20 minutes.

4. Remove the pan from the machine and proof at the same temperature until the dough rises about ½ inch above the pan top (2 to 3 hours at room temperature; 1½ to 2 hours at 85°).

5. If your machine has a bake only cycle, return the pan to the machine and program the cycle to bake at 375° for 50 to 60 minutes. If not, move the pan to your preheated oven at 375° and bake for 45 minutes. Remove the loaf from the pan and cool on a wire rack.

WILD CULTURES FROM
SOURDOUGHS INTERNATIONAL

When I returned from the Middle East, I had a refrigerator full of Middle Eastern and European wild sourdough cultures. I marveled at their vitality every time I opened the door and saw them waiting to be fed. I wondered if anyone could ever be as enchanted with those cultures as I was. How to find out? I couldn't imagine sending the fermenting mixtures through the mail. Instead, I experimented with drying them at temperatures low enough to preserve their viability, yet warm enough to dry them completely. Then I added water to reconstitute the mixture. They survived the drying, but when I poured a sourdough culture onto a baking sheet and let it dry, it formed a rock-hard slab that was almost impossible to break, grind, or mix with water. It took months of testing, but by carefully regulating the drying temperatures and adding flour at the right moment, I managed to encapsulate the delicate yeasts in a cocoon of flour that dissolves easily in water and starts them off to bake for another century or so.

What do you name a company that grows and sells wild sourdough cultures? Ed's Breads didn't quite do it. My most creative thinking usually occurs about 2 A.M., and that's when Sourdoughs International popped in and stayed.

With a company name, a book, and eight priceless wild sourdough cultures, we were off and running (running scared, that is). I thought it would be a great challenge and a lot of fun to market and distribute the book and cultures. There was only one problem. I hated sales. I shall never forget my first sales call. I knocked timidly on the office door of the owner of Boise's Book

Shop. She was busy and I was an interruption. I left with an order for ten books, a warm glow, and the memory of a very gracious lady. Since then I've met thousands of people throughout the world who are as committed as I am to the rebirth and preservation of the best breads man has ever known. But I still hate selling!

Along the way I acquired two additional cultures, one from Russia and another from Finland. Then I made an unexpected acquisition. For almost thirty years I had studied the research and publications of Leo Kline and W. T. Sugihara, the two California researchers who identified and reported on the organisms of San Francisco sourdough. But I never had an opportunity to obtain the culture that has produced the San Francisco bread for well over a century. That is, until 1997. My benefactor must remain anonymous, but that culture has, in many ways, changed the way I think about sourdoughs. In fact, it bears a large responsibility for this new book and the methods with which I am fast becoming acquainted and passing on to you. Naturally we named it the Original San Francisco.

Our World Cultures

Is one sourdough really different from another? Of course! They differ in flavor, sourness, and speed and strength of leavening. The true purist judges sourdoughs primarily on their flavor and then on their sourness. Evaluating sourdough flavor is not quite as sophisticated as wine tasting (there are no "stemmy sourdoughs"), but it may be close. I sometimes think most of us have eaten enough commercial "sourdough" with its additives of vinegar and acetic acid to believe that all sourdough should taste that sour. Nothing could be further from the truth. Having said that, I should acknowledge that on occasion a baker will complain that one of our cultures is too sour.

Breads of the Middle East
In many parts of the Middle East, bread baking is virtually unchanged from its inception ten thousand years ago. These ancient bakeries are as likely to be found in the middle of metropolitan Cairo as in the smallest and most remote desert village. They are usually secluded on village streets in thick mud-walled

buildings that conceal ovens developed eons ago. And it is very difficult to gain entry. The proprietors are suspicious of any non-Arab seeking information. The language barrier adds to the difficulty, but even with a native guide we faced rebuff at every turn.

It was in this environment that we sought and found our sourdough cultures from antiquity. Gaining access was an achievement, leaving with a sample of unbaked dough a triumph. Tact, diplomacy, sign language, pantomime, and a smile sometimes accomplished what often seemed beyond reach. Getting those precious samples of dried, unidentifiable white substances through airports and multiple custom inspections was the culmination of each adventure. From our successes we selected four cultures to represent the Middle East. Two are from Egypt, the acknowledged home of humankind's first bakery; one is from Bahrain, the ancient Garden of Eden and an early crossroads of trade routes between the East, the Middle East, and Europe; and one is from Saudi Arabia, because no collection of breads from the Middle East would be complete without a sourdough culture from the desert kingdom.

The Giza Sourdough

The Giza culture is very likely the oldest one we offer. It comes from the rich Nile agricultural area isolated for centuries by a desert on one side and the Red Sea on the other—ideal circumstances to protect a culture from contamination. It has a moderate to slow leavening speed with a mild flavor and moderate sourness. It is not suitable for bread machines except when using a dough cycle. It is an excellent culture for flatbreads and pitas.

We met Hamid, a gregarious taxi driver, in Cairo. He spoke English and claimed to have spent four years driving a cab in New York City. Driving in Cairo is an incredible experience. With a population of sixteen million, there seems to be a car for every person and absolutely no place to drive, park, or dodge. Hamid did all those things while talking and looking us straight in the eye as he barreled from one destination to another.

It took a while to convince Hamid that we wanted to go to an old bakery, not a new one, and we didn't want to buy bread at all. We wanted to visit and tour and talk to bakers. And we wanted some dough. Not bread, but dough. And we wanted to do it all in Giza. So off we went, with Hamid looking us in the eye and explaining that what we wanted might not be too easy. Egyptian bakers, he said, are not eager to have visitors, especially in the old bakeries we wanted to see. In addition, because of increasing efforts to improve the sanitation of all food establishments, taking pictures and asking questions in an old bakery might intimidate the bakers. Con artist that Hamid was, he was unable to get us past the front door of the first and second bakeries. Finally, it was my wife who got us into what looked like the oldest bakery in Giza, situated almost between the paws of the Sphinx. A goat was tied in the doorway. She made friends with it first. A ten-year-old boy, who was obviously very attached to the goat, was her next conquest. He worked in the bakery and was apparently the son of the proprietor. Did the lady want to come in? He could arrange it. With our youthful guide, we cautiously explored that ancient bakery.

There were three small, dingy rooms. The dough, a mixture of flour, water, and the previous day's culture, was mixed in one room. The flatbreads were formed in another, and the oven was in the third. The hand-turned mixer was the only mechanical equipment. As the dough came from the mixer, it was pummeled by a baker until its consistency met his satisfaction. Round flatbreads about ten inches in diameter were formed by hand and allowed to "rest" for thirty to sixty minutes. They were then placed on a long paddle, thrust into the oven, and, with a quick twist, deposited on the oven's hot floor. Within a minute, they suddenly puffed violently, broke into a brief flash of flame, and, after another minute, were removed with a deft maneuver of the paddle. The bread was sold at the door as fast as it came from the oven. We could have purchased bread with the crowd at the door without difficulty. When Hamid explained that it was dough we wanted, the owner needed an explanation. What was said is uncertain, but from the smiles and raised eyebrows, I suspect our sanity was being discussed. At any rate, we received a plastic bag of dough—and a flatbread—with the compliments of the owner.

THE RED SEA SOURDOUGH

When we found this culture in 1984, Hurghada on the Red Sea existed much as it had in ancient times, and so did the sourdough we discovered there. The

Hurghada we saw no longer exists today. In its place are high-rise buildings, condominiums, resort hotels, and commercial yeast. This is one of our faster-leavening cultures, suitable for most bread machines. It has a mild flavor and sourness. It works well for any bread recipe made by hand.

Hurghada proved to be everything we had hoped: narrow, winding streets; squat mud-walled buildings; shuttered windows; Moslem dress. The streets were dotted with small shops selling vegetables, incense, and crafts. It was all *ancient* Egypt. We finally identified the town bakery by the rows of bread loaves spread on the street to rise in the hot afternoon sun. *"Men kam?"* (How much?) I asked, pointing to a stack of fresh-baked breads. *"Ashra"* came the answer. The negotiation completed, I bit into the bread. "Hmmm, *kuais"* (good). Then I was stuck. I had almost exhausted my limited supply of Arabic. How to ask for some unbaked dough? I tried a smile and a gesture. No response. Then I lifted my camera and pantomimed taking a picture. The reaction was immediate and emphatic: *"la, la"* (no, no). Suddenly, I was not only unwelcome, but I was being asked to leave, and in no uncertain terms. At that moment, someone in the crowd stepped forward. "Can I help you?" came in welcome English. I explained my desire to obtain some unbaked dough, and he passed the words on to the proprietor, who anxiously eyed the gathering crowd, assessing his next move. He paused, then motioned me forward. The crisis was over and we entered another scene from Egypt's ancient past.

The interior was dark and composed of many small rooms lighted only from small, high windows. Each room was designated for a specific function. In one, flour and water were mixed in what looked like a cement mixer turned by hand. A five-gallon bucket of "starter" from the previous day was added. That was the dough. Neither salt nor sugar was used. The dough was then divided among several rooms, and, depending on the room, shaped into loaves, flatbreads, or rolls. Some loaves were allowed to rise, others were baked unleavened. The "production lines" flowed toward a large clay oven. We admired everything and the owner beamed with pride. I doubt that he ever understood our interest in his dough, but when asked, although obviously puzzled, he filled our small plastic bags.

THE BAHRAIN SOURDOUGH

The Bahrain culture is one of our more inherently sour cultures. Remember that all sourdoughs will become more sour if proofing times are increased. The caveat is that the Bahrain will be somewhat more sour whether the proofing time is short or long. It is slow leavening and unsuitable for bread machines except those with a dough cycle. It is suitable for all bread recipes made by hand.

The history of Dilmun-Bahrain abounds with myths and names from antiquity: the Assyrian Empire, the Babylonians, Persia, Alexander the Great. It was known as the place of immortality, the Garden of Eden. Bahrain's strategic location and unusual water supply made it a center of trade more than four thousand years ago. Today, it is an archipelago of some thirty-three islands located approximately halfway down the Gulf of Arabia. The name means "two seas," in reference to the many freshwater springs that arise off-shore and on the islands.

The old Bahrain bakeries make flatbreads almost exclusively. The ovens are dome shaped and heated with wood. The baker places the uncooked flat-bread on a cushion rounded to match the inside curve of the oven dome. With a deft move, he slaps the bread on the hot, inner surface of the oven. It glows and puffs briefly and the baker then expertly removes it.

We were met in Bahrain bakeries with the same suspicion that we experienced throughout the Middle East. As long as negotiations were confined to buying bread, visitors were tolerated, but any attempt to go further was resisted or refused outright. Most Western tourists in Bahrain buy food in the security of hotels, where they have more confidence in the integrity of the water and cuisine. Our inquiries at ancient bakeries immediately caused suspicion.

We were refused permission to enter bakeries several times, but finally, relying on basic Arab courtesy and the inherent curiosity of children, we succeeded. My wife struck up a smiling contest with a handsome youngster and offered his parent, who happened to work in an adjacent bakery, a Polaroid picture. We exchanged pleasantries and eventually gained access.

Although our presence in this bakery was tolerated grudgingly, we had no difficulty getting some unbaked dough. They surely thought our tastes peculiar, but from an ancient bakery in the land of Dilmun we acquired a bit of immortal history that may date into the distant past.

THE SAUDI ARABIAN SOURDOUGH

If you want to taste a sourdough with a different flavor, this is the one. It leavens at a moderate rate, is not generally suited to bread machines for that reason, and produces an absolutely out-of-this-world Arab pita bread—the best I've ever experienced.

Saudi Arabia is a rapidly changing country that has advanced two thousand years in one lifetime. For this reason, it presents an intriguing mixture of the old with the new. Most Bedouins, or desert Arabs, live now as they have always lived, in tents in the desert, tending their camels and goats. Even modern city dwellers retain much of the culture of the past.

The breads of the desert are the same today as they were hundreds of years ago. The Bedouin sourdough cultures fed Mohammed, Lawrence of Arabia, and King Abdul Aziz. This was the culture we wanted for our desert breads. But where to find a bakery in the desert? The hospital I worked in was built fifteen miles from Riyadh to supply modern medical care to the Saudi Arabian National Guard and their families. The Guard, all Bedouins, is charged with protecting the king and his family. They settled near the hospital and brought with them their shops and souks. One was a bakery that produced a flatbread straight from the desert. This operation, not half a mile from the hospital, in a solitary, dilapidated building beside the road, was best known for its spit-roasted chicken. It was irreverently known as Chicken Charlie's, and it took us a year to realize that desert sourdough had searched us out, instead of us finding it.

Breads of Europe

The origin of Western civilization was somewhere in the Middle East, and the production of grains evolved in those areas and gradually spread northward to Europe. For hundreds of years, however, the dominant grain in Europe was rye, not wheat. In much of the developing world, rye was regarded as a weed, but in Europe it was the staff of life. As a result, recipes from the Germanic lands are heavily endowed with rye flavor.

Most sourdough cultures do not readily ferment rye flours. The amino acids and carbohydrates of the "weed" apparently require a special and hardy yeast. For this reason, we were especially pleased to find a sourdough culture in Innsbruck, Austria, that had obviously adapted to this task.

The Austrian Sourdough

This is the sourdough that almost changed my life, and I have some regrets about that. I'll bet the thirty years I could have served in a Saudi jail for its possession would have been material for a best-seller. The Innsbruck culture evolved in Austria. It doesn't leaven very rapidly. In some programmable machines you can usually maximize the last rising cycle and get by with a fairly heavy rye recipe. I recommend the culture for any recipe containing rye flour if made by hand.

We were on our way to Oberkochen in what was then West Germany, where I was to learn to operate an electron microscope. On our way we took a detour through the lovely, medieval town of Innsbruck. By pure serendipity, we found ourselves staring through a bakery window with a sign proclaiming Sauerbraten! The women tending the counter spoke not a word of English and we hardly a word of German. Hand signals worked wonders, and we pantomimed our way to a partially underground room where three bakers were preparing the day's bread. One spoke enough English to confirm that, indeed, they saved a portion of the dough each day to start the next day's mix. Without even looking, we had found a classic European sourdough. I dried the Innsbruck culture and wrapped it in aluminum foil.

Never in my worst dreams could I have imagined what would happen when I tried to take it back to Saudi Arabia. All was well until we got to Jeddah on our way to Riyadh. You have to go through Saudi customs to believe what happens in this process. Your luggage is searched for contraband, including alcohol, drugs, and pornography (which might include a package of panty hose with a picture of women's legs). The metal detectors are set to be extremely sensitive. There is no mistaking the seriousness of the occasion. Violate a Saudi law and they may put you in jail and throw away the key. At the very least, you could be detained for twelve or more hours at the airport. The consequences are multiplied by the indifference of the foreign embassies.

I tripped one of the metal detectors and knew instantly that I was in serious trouble. The armed Saudi guard was taking no chances, and I was fast running out of ideas. How do you explain a packet of white, granular material to an airport security guard in a country where drug smuggling is so serious it doesn't even occur, especially when he doesn't understand your language and you don't understand his? Instantly a young guard motioned me to step aside and empty my pockets. I knew, without a doubt, that my aluminum foil packet of sourdough was the culprit, but I emptied my pockets of everything metal, hoping I could get under the detection level of the instrument. It didn't work. I tripped it again and again. By now I had the guard's full attention. What had looked at first like a routine pocket of change now required an explanation. The expression on my face didn't help as I tried to unscramble my brains and come up with an explanation. I finally tried, "Oh, maybe it's my lunch wrapper," and fished out what remotely resembled a very dry piece of bread wrapped in foil. I had no idea how much he understood of what I said. At that moment Allah must have smiled: some unlucky soul behind me tripped the detector. The guard glared at the interruption, made a quick decision, and motioned for me to pick up my possessions and go. I fled! Needless to say, I have never wrapped anything else in aluminum foil if there is a metal detector in my future.

The French Sourdough

Most of us are unaware that authentic sourdoughs in France are almost extinct. French bakers lost no time in converting to commercial yeast, and the real stuff has been hard to find for years with a few notable exceptions, perhaps Lionel Poilâne being the outstanding example. This culture leavens well but not quickly, has a good flavor, is not overly sour, and does better when the bread is made by hand than in a machine. It works very well with the French Bread recipe on page 66.

No collection of European cultures would be complete without a representative from France, where bread has been an important factor in politics and survival since the French Revolution. While not as ancient as the breads of the Middle East, sourdough breads have sustained the French people since the Dark Ages. The very term *French bread* conjures an image of a sourdough bread familiar throughout most of the world.

The French are so possessive of their sourdough that we felt we had acquired a national treasure when we finally obtained a culture. Everyone in

France seems absolutely convinced that there is only one French sourdough and is equally determined that it not emigrate to the United States. We explained our mission to our taxi driver and told him about our collection of cultures from the Middle East. He was entranced. For a small, undetermined fee he would introduce us to a baker, his uncle. He brought the car to a screeching stop in front of a sidewalk cafe that was attached to an unimposing bakery. We took a table for four and ordered wine and bread. It wasn't long before the taxi driver returned with his gray-haired, portly uncle, the personification of a French baker. Another bottle of wine appeared. "And what do you think of the sourdough you are enjoying with the wine?" he asked. When we left two hours later, we had the French sourdough culture.

THE FINNISH SOURDOUGH

This is not a fast leavener, but it is a strong one. By that, I mean it reaches its peak leavening in four hours or so and is still at the same level after twelve hours of proofing—in marked contrast to the Russian culture described below. It has a distinctive flavor that I still haven't found the appropriate words to describe and a rather sour aftertaste. It is not a good culture for use in a bread machine.

When our son, Keith, a biochemist and avid sourdough baker, made a business trip to Finland, he was programmed to bring back a sourdough culture. He had to go to small villages and fight the language barrier, but he did come back with the culture and a book on Finnish breads.

THE RUSSIAN SOURDOUGH

This is the culture that will convince anyone that all sourdoughs are not the same. It is the fastest wild sourdough I have ever seen. If I use this culture on a daily basis, which I often do, it reaches its peak leavening rate in less than an hour and a half to two hours after I've taken it out of the refrigerator. It leavens a loaf of bread in the same time or less. So why use anything else? There are several reasons. The culture is intrinsically mild in flavor and sourness and it exhausts the nutrients in flour, becoming semidormant almost as fast as it reaches its peak leavening. For full flavor development it must proof overnight or twelve hours like any other culture. By the end of that time, however, the wild yeasts are sound asleep. If the loaves are formed at this point, they won't even start to rise for at least an hour and a half. This is no problem if your schedule permits, as mine usually does. I simply add a cup of flour to the dough after it has proofed about ten hours. This gives the yeasts a wakeup call and gets them working at full steam by the time the dough has been proofing for a total of twelve hours, which is when the loaves are formed. Because of its leavening speed, it is clearly the best culture for most bread machines. Plus, a lot of bakers consider that mild flavor an asset.

Russian-born Tanya Bevin contacted us in her attempt to bake breads as she remembered them. Her experience with commercial loaves was a culture shock, and she came to us desperately looking for an Old World starter. We gave her the Finnish culture. She lived in Seattle and worked as a tour guide to Russia. With her background in science and frequent trips to Russia, she seemed the ideal person to get a Russian culture. She brought back two from small villages north of Moscow. One is the most active sourdough culture we have seen.

Breads of North America
THE YUKON SOURDOUGH

It is a mistake to overemphasize the importance of Yukon sourdoughs in the broad spectrum of North American breads, for they are mere fledglings. To be sure, this culture is symbolic of the legends and present-day image of sourdough in this country. Yet it is easy to forget that when the Pilgrims landed in 1620, they brought their sourdoughs with them. In the ensuing years, these cultures spread across the continent and made our bread for almost 230 years before gold was discovered in the West. That heritage of sourdough has left priceless sourdough cultures from Maine to New Mexico, from Florida to Alaska, and in spite of the convenience of commercial yeast, thousands of bread addicts and experts still choose the product made with sourdough.

Our Yukon culture passed from hand to hand directly from that source of unquestioned authenticity, a Yukon prospector. It came to me by way of a medical-school classmate who ended up in Saudi Arabia practicing radiology in the same hospital in which I was a pathologist. We hadn't seen each other in twenty years, but it didn't take long for us to discover our mutual weakness—sourdough. He convinced his physician father to dry the Yukon culture and send us a few crumbs in a letter. The Yukon is moderately fast to leaven but slow for most bread machines except on the dough cycle. It is also moderately sour with a "Yukon" flavor. I have a host of friends that swear it is the only culture for real sourdough flapjacks.

THE ORIGINAL SAN FRANCISCO SOURDOUGH

In 1997 we had the good fortune to acquire the culture considered the authentic San Francisco sourdough. Extensive research published in 1970 identified for the first time the wild yeast that makes this sourdough bread rise and the bacteria that produces its flavor. The researchers developed methods to permit commercial bakers to duplicate the process everywhere. We now offer this culture to the home baker. The wild yeast was originally classified as a strain of *Saccharomyces exiguus,* called *Torulopsis holmii.* It was subsequently reclassified as *Candida milleri.* Now, as I was writing these words, I just received information from a reader of our newsletter that the classification has been changed again and is now *Candida humilis.* No, the organism hasn't changed, just the name. The bacteria is *Lactobacillus sanfrancisco.* The two organisms thrive in a symbiotic relationship that has protected the culture from contamination from other yeasts and bacteria for over a century of baking. It is this symbiosis that, contrary to widespread mythology, will prevent contamination from organisms in your environment. The researchers found that "it seems apparent that this system would not work if baker's yeast were teamed with the sour dough bacteria."

This culture has become our favorite for bake tests and is also the favorite of most of those who have received it from us. It allows long fermentations, so bread can be mild to very flavorful and sour.

Breads of South Africa

Sourdoughs International is always interested in new, good international sourdough cultures. I receive several letters every year from home bakers extolling the virtues of their prized collections and sometimes offering one for me to test and perhaps add to the collection described here. With ten more or less dormant cultures already demanding attention in my refrigerators, I usually respond with interest, but a "no thanks." But would you believe a culture that grows in 100 percent whole wheat and leavens 100 percent whole-wheat doughs better and faster than it leavens 100 percent white flour doughs? Well, neither did I until the following e-mail arrived:

> I am e-mailing from the other side of the world—Cape Town in South Africa to be exact, and I am proud to say I have a culture that happily rises at temperatures down to 18°C (that's 64°F), gives a lovely strong flavour and most importantly with several ravenous buddies, it really "fills up the corners." The starter is pretty tough, resilient, and wakes up easily. My point to all this is: Would you be interested in a starter portion, and how would I go about drying out the yeast in order to post it to you?

At that point just being from South Africa made that culture interesting, so I asked for more information.

Back came the answer:

> I have a suspicion that you are hoping for a long, detailed account showing how this starter has been passed from generation to generation down through the ages until I got it! Well, sorry, no can do there, but here's what I can tell you. I have made a culture before, and indeed I have made my own bread for close to five years. Then for some reason, I threw the culture out and started eating "cardboard" again. However, I started wanting flavour in my bread and the new culture was created. What I like about this culture is that it is very flexible with regard to rising times and it can create a very strongly flavoured loaf. I always use pure whole wheat, no unbleached white flour available here, or at least not easily so. To summarize: The culture is easygoing. Any mix of flour (though it has been trained on whole wheat), somewhat wet or somewhat dry dough, cool temperatures or warm will work. The taste has the potential to become very powerful, when fermentation is left for eight to ten hours. The culture becomes active quickly when taken out of the fridge. What else can I say, Ed—it is a bachelor's friend (second only to the washing machine).

Well, this certainly was not a heritage culture, but it sounded like it had a most unusual wild yeast and lactobacillus from South Africa. I could hardly wait to get my hands on it and said so. A ball of moist culture surrounded by a somewhat granular whole-wheat mixture arrived in about ten days. The total package weighed about three pounds, which was largely due to the surrounding whole wheat. I pinched off about a third of the culture ball, mixed it with some warm water and fed it some of the whole wheat. By the next morning at 80°F it was showing signs of activity and had an almost acrid odor. Over the next ten days, I split the culture, feeding one-half only whole wheat, the other only white flour. Those South African organisms actually leaven whole wheat better than they leaven white flour.

The flavor of the whole-wheat loaves was nutty and different. Interestingly, the taste of the white flour loaves was also exceptional, but clearly different from the whole wheat. Recipes for those two breads are in the recipe section. The possibilities for different combinations of the two flours and other ingredients appear endless.

For information on ordering these cultures, contact:

Sourdoughs International
P.O. Box 670
Cascade, ID 83611
Tel: 208-382-4828
Fax: 208-382-3129
Web site: www.sourdo.com

APPENDIX

The Consistency Template

If you have sensitive fingers that know when the consistency of a dough is just right, you can forget all about this template. I think the information from my fingers stops at about my elbows so I use the template frequently, especially when I'm testing new recipes.

Whenever you use a different culture (liquid or sponge) or when you want to make more or less dough than specified in a recipe, the amount of flour and water obviously changes. The template gives you a good estimate of how much flour or water to add or subtract. It is based on a few assumptions, which are hardly cast in concrete so they vary from time to time and probably differ a bit from my kitchen to yours. The assumptions listed below are what I use with my cultures, my flour, and my environment. The calculations are just guidelines and when the figures come out with two decimal points, I round them off to the nearest quarter of a cup. That I can measure. Some of us find templates of this sort a little confusing so I have added here the thought process I usually go through to make this thing work.

The first assumption is that the ideal dough consistency is based on 63 percent flour and 37 percent water. This template will not help you with ingredients or flours that slurp up a lot more water than white bread flour. These include bulgur and some rye and barley flours, to name a few. Then you just have to wing it.

My Assumptions

- A liquid culture is about 48 percent flour, 52 percent water.

- A sponge culture is about 65 percent flour, 35 percent water.

- A cup of either a liquid culture or a sponge culture weighs about 9 ounces.

- A cup of flour weighs about 5 ounces.

- A cup of water weighs 8 ounces (and that one you can use to check your scale).

I start by making two decisions: What kind of culture and how much of it? In the example below, I chose ½ cup (4.5 ounces) of a sponge culture. The next decision is the amount of dough desired. For two 1½ pound loaves I will need 52 ounces of dough (about 4 ounces are lost in baking).

So the first line of the template shows how much flour is in the culture, .65 x 4.5 = 2.93 ounces; and water, .35 x 4.5 = 1.57. The last line shows how much flour is desired in the dough, .63 x 52 = 32.76 ounces; and water, .37 x 52 = 19.24. By subtracting the amount of flour and water already in the culture from the amount desired in the dough, I determine how much I need to add of both in the recipe. For flour, 32.76 ounces minus 2.93 = 29.83 ounces. Since 1 cup of flour weighs 5 ounces, 29.83 ounces divided by 5 equals 5.97 cups of flour which I round to 6. For water 19.24 ounces minus 1.57 = 17.67 ounces of water, divided by 8 equals 2.21 cups which I round to 2¼ cups. Simple, huh?

CONSISTENCY TEMPLATE (IN OUNCES AND CUPS)

	FLOUR	WATER	TOTAL
½ cup sponge	2.93 oz	1.57 oz	4.4 oz
5.97 cups flour	29.83	29.83	
2.21 cups water		17.67	17.67
Totals	32.76	19.24	52.0 oz
Percentage	63%	37%	

1 ounce = 28.35 grams
1 cup (liquid) = 261 milliliters

SELECTED SOURCES

FOR BULGUR:
Sunnyland Mills
4469 East Annadale Ave.
Fresno, CA 93725-2221
Tel: (559) 233-4983
Fax: (559) 233-6431

FOR FLAX:
The Pizzey Mill
P.O. Box 132
Angusville, MB R0J 0A0 Canada
Tel: (800) 804-6433
Fax: (204) 773-2317
Web site: www.pizzeys.com

FOR ORGANIC FLOURS:
Certified Foods, Inc.
1055 Montague Ave.
San Leandro, CA 94577-4311
Tel: (510) 483-1177
Fax: (510) 483-1776

FOR FLOURS IN GENERAL:
Gold Mine Natural Food Co.
3419 Hancock St.
San Diego, CA 92110-4307
Tel: (800) 475-3663
Fax: (619) 296-9756
E-mail: goldmine@1x.netcom.com

FOR SPELT:
Purity Foods, Inc.
2871 West Jolly Rd.
Okemose, MI 48864
Tel: (517) 351-9231
Fax: (517) 351-9391

FOR SOY ISOFLAVONES:
Schouten USA, Inc.
330 Edinborough Way
Minneapolis, MN 55435
Tel: (952) 920-7700
Fax: (952) 920-7704
E-mail: soylife@schoutenusa.com
Web site: www.soylife.com

BIBLIOGRAPHY

Barnett, J. A., R. W. Payne, and D. Yarrow. *Yeast: Characteristics and Identification* (3rd edition), New York: Cambridge University Press, 2000.

Chelminski, Rudolph. "Anyway You Slice It, A Poilâne Loaf Is Real French Bread." *Smithsonian* (January 1995): 51–57.

Kline, Leo, and T. F. Sugihara. "Microorganisms of the San Francisco Sour Dough Bread Process. II. Isolation and Characterization of Undescribed Bacterial Species Responsible for the Souring Activity." *Applied Microbiology 21* (1971): 459–65.

Kline, Leo, T. F. Sugihara, and Linda Bele McCready. "Nature of the San Francisco Sour Dough French Bread Process. I. Mechanics of the Process." *The Bakers Digest* (1970): 48–50.

McCay, Clive M., and Jeanette B. McCay. *The Cornell Bread Book.* New York: Dover Publications, Inc., 1980.

Roberts, David. "After 4500 Years, Rediscovering Egypt's Bread Baking Technology." *National Geographic* (January 1995): 32–35.

Sugihara, T. F., Leo Kline, and M. W. Miller. "Microorganisms of the San Francisco Sour Dough Bread Process. I. Yeasts Responsible for the Leavening Action." *Applied Microbiology 21* (1971): 456–58.

Wing, Daniel, and Alan Scott. *The Bread Builders, Hearth Loaves and Masonry Ovens.* White River Junction, VT: Chelsea Green Publishing House, 1999.

INDEX

Italics indicate pages with bread machine recipes.

Activation, 39–41
American Institute of Baking, 23, 56
Anise rye bread, *174*
Applesauce pancakes, 154
Arrowhead Mills, 18, 21
Artisan bakers, xiii, 5–6
Austrian rye pancakes, 155
Austrian sourdough culture, 70, 191–92
Austrian spelt bread, 104
Austrian wheat-rye bread, 57

Bagels, 114
Bahrain sourdough culture, 80, 133,
    189–90
Baking
  doneness and, 47–48
  steps in, 44–48
Baking pans, 37
Baking sheets, 37
Baking stones, 38
Banana batter bread, 145
Batter breads, 143–52
  banana, 145
  basic, 144
  cheese, 146
  corn, 147
  cranberry-huckleberry, 148
  dill, 149

  limpa, 150
  nut-raisin, 151
  whole-wheat, 152
Beer bread, malt, 75
Bevin, Tanya, 194
Black bread, Tanya's peasant, 90, *183*
Bleached flours, 12
Blueberries
  cranberry rye, 64
  waffles, 159
Bowls, 36
Braided egg bread, 122–23
Bread
  chemicals added to, xii–xiii, 2
  decline in quality of, xii
  history of, xi–xii, 1
  industrial production of, xii–xiii, 2
Bread machines
  activating and culture preparation, 169
  ancient Egyptian bread molds vs., 38
  bake only cycle, 169–170
  dough consistency, 171
  dough cycle, 171–72
  good results from, 38, 167–68
  models of, 170
  process for, 170–72
  proofing, 169
  recipes for, *172–83*

Breadsticks, 115–16
Bulgur, 23–25
Bulgur breads
   basic, 110–11
   whole-grain, 112
Buns, hamburger, 132
Butterflake rolls, 127–28
Buttermilk waffles, 160

Caraway crunches, 117
Caraway rye bread, 58
Caraway rye bread with soy, 106
Caraway spelt bread, 105
Certified Foods, 16, 18
Cheese breads
   basic, 59
   batter, 146
   onion-, 60
Christmas bread, German, 69
Cinnamon-raisin nut bread, 61–62
Consistency, dough, 44, 171, 200–201
Cooling racks, 37
Corn batter bread, 147
Cracked wheat
   about, 13, 71
   and graham bread, 71
Cranberries, 32
   -blueberry rye, 64
   -huckleberry batter bread, 148
   -nut sourdough, 63
Crust texture, 48
Cultures
   activating dried, 39–41
   capturing your own, 8–9, 10–11
   caring for heritage, 48–49
   commercial yeast added to, 3
   containers for, 36
   contamination of, 40, 48–49
   European, 190–94
   feeding stock, 41
   leavening power of, 167–68
   liquid, 40, 41–42, 43, 51
   mail-order sources of, 184–97

   maintaining and reactivating stock,
      43–44
   Middle Eastern, 185–90
   milk added to, 6, 9, 30
   North American, 194–95
   preparation of, 35, 41–42
   research on, 3–7
   South African, 195–97
   sponge, 42, 43, 51
   washing, 40–41, 50–51
Curran, Steve, 16

Date bread, 65, *178*
Dill batter bread, 149
Dinner rolls, 129–30
Do-good loaf, 26, 91
Doneness, 47–48
Dough consistency, 44, 171, 200–201
Durum breads, 94–98
   rye, 95
   sunflower, 96
   sunflower with soy, 98, 107
   world, 97
Durum flour, 17–18

Egg bread, braided, 122–23
Elias, Dr. Elias, 17
English muffins, 124–25
Equipment, 35–39
European sourdough cultures, 190–94

Fats, 31
Fermentation, 4, 6
Finnish rye bread, 68
Finnish sourdough culture, 68, 193
Flatbreads
   khubz arabi (Arab bread), 134–35
   khubz saj (thin bread), 136
   mafrooda, 137
   saluf, 138
Flavor, 4, 50
Flax, 21–23

Flax breads, 99–101
    prairie, 99
    pumpernickel rye, 100
    whole-wheat, 101
Flax Council of Canada, 23
Flour
    choosing, 15–16
    comparisons of, 14–15
    durum, 17–18
    kamut, 18–19
    organic, 16–17
    soy, 26–30
    wheat bread, 11–16
French bread, 66–67
French Meadow Bakery, xiii
French sourdough culture, 192–93

German Christmas bread, 69
German rye bread, 70
Gilbertson, Arlen, 17, 18
Gingerbread waffles, 161
Giza sourdough culture, 186–87
Gluten, 13
Gordon, Lynn, xiii
Graham and cracked-wheat bread, 71

Hamburger buns, 132
Ham waffles, 162
Hard wheat, 11
Herb breads
    basic, 72
    rosemary, 86
    spelt, 102
Hilbeh, 139
Huckleberry-cranberry batter bread, 148

Interstate Bakeries Corporation, xii–xiii
Isoflavones, 28–29

Kamut bread, 109
Kamut flour, 18–19
Khubz arabi (Arab bread), 134–35
Khubz saj (thin bread), 136

Kline, Leo, 4–5, 44, 185
Kneading, 45–46
Kosnopfl, Wilhelm, 19

La Cloche
    description of, 38, 47, 73
    sourdough, 73–74
Lactobacilli, xii, 4–5, 6, 9, 10
Light Swedish limpa, 76–78, *182*
Limpas
    batter bread, 150
    light Swedish, 76–78, *182*
Loaves, forming, 46–47

Mafrooda, 137
Malt beer bread, 75
Maple pancakes, 156
McCay, Clive, 26–28, 91
Middle Eastern sourdough cultures,
    185–90
Milk, 6, 9, 26–27, 30
Milling, 12
Muffins
    English, 124–25
    whole-wheat, 126
Multigrain bread, 87

North American sourdough cultures,
    194–95
Nut breads
    banana batter, 145
    cinnamon-raisin, 61–62
    cranberry-, 63
    date, 65
    raisin batter, 151
    Saudi date, *178*

Oatmeal bread, 79, *176*
Oils, 31
Olive bread, onion-, 80–81
Onion breads
    cheese-, 60
    olive-, 80–81
Organic flour, 16–17

Original San Francisco sourdough culture, 16, 29, 56, 167–68, *177*, 185, 195
Orlando, Michael, 24, 25
Ovens, 36

Pancakes, 153–57
  applesauce, 154
  Austrian rye, 155
  maple, 156
  Yukon flapjacks, 157
Parker House rolls, 129–30
Pasteur, Louis, xii, 2
Personalization, 32–33
Phytoestrogens, 28
Pizza, 118–19
Pizzey, Linda and Glenn, 21–23
Poppyseed rolls, 131
Potato bread, 82
Pretzels, salted, 120–21
Proofing, 39–44
  boxes, 35
  temperatures, 169
Pumpernickel breads
  basic, 83
  with flax, 100
Pumpernickel flour, 21

Quinn, Bob, 18

Raisin breads
  bran cereal sourdough, 84
  cinnamon nut, 61–62
  German Christmas, 69
  nut batter, 151
  rosemary, 86
  rye, 85
Red Sea sourdough culture, 187–88
Retarding, 43, 169
Rocky Mountain Flour Milling, 16
Rolls
  butterflake, 127–28
  dinner, 129–30
  Parker House, 129–30
  poppyseed, 131

Rosemary bread, 86
Russian sourdough culture, 92, 96, 101, 193–94
Rye breads. *See also* Pumpernickel breads
  anise, 174
  Austrian wheat-, 57
  caraway, 58, *175*
  caraway with soy, 106
  cranberry-blueberry, 64
  durum, 95
  Finnish, 68
  German, 70
  light Swedish limpa, 76–78, *182*
  malt beer, 75
  pancakes, Austrian, 155
  raisin, 85
  sour cream, 88, *179*
  waffles, 163
Rye flour, 20–21

Saccharomyces cerevisiae, xii, 3
Salt, 31
Salted pretzels, 120–21
Saluf, 138
San Francisco sourdough bread, 4–5, 56, *177*
San Francisco sourdough culture. *See* Original San Francisco sourdough culture
Saudi Arabian sourdough culture, 65, 133, 134, 190
Saudi date bread, *178*
Scales, 38–39
Schouten USA, 28–30
Scott, Allen, 36
Seven-grain-cereal sourdough, 87
Soft wheat, 11
Sour cream rye bread, 88, *179*
Sour cream waffles, 164
Sourdoughs International, 8, 184–97
South African sourdough culture, 140–42, 195–97

Soy, 25–30
  caraway rye bread with, 106
  do-good loaf, 91
  durum sunflower bread with, 98, 107
  world bread with, 108
Spelt breads, 102–5
  Austrian, 104
  basic, 103
  caraway, 105
  herb, 102
  sunflower, *181*
Spelt flour, 19–20, 104
Spring wheat, 11–12
Starters. *See* Cultures
Stollens, 69
Sugar, 32
Sugihara, T. F., 4–5, 44, 185
Sunflower seed breads
  basic, 89, *180*
  durum, 96
  durum with soy, 98, 107
  spelt, *181*
Sunnyland Mills, 24, 25
Swedish limpa, light, 76–78, *182*
Sweeteners, 32

Tanya's peasant black bread, 90, *183*
Texture, 48, 50
Thermometers, 37
"Traditional" sourdough, definition of,
  xi–xii

Unbleached flours, 12
Utensils, 36

Vanderliet, Joseph, 16, 18
Van Leewenhoek, Anton, 2
Vital Gluten, 21
Vita-Spelt, 20

Waffles, 158–66
  blueberry, 159
  buttermilk, 160
  gingerbread, 161

  ham, 162
  rye, 163
  sour cream, 164
  whole-wheat, 165
  Yukon, 166
Walnuts. *See* Nut breads
Water, 31
Wheat bread flour, 11–16
Wheat germ, 26–27
Wheat gluten, 21
White breads
  do-good loaf, 91
  herb, 72
  oatmeal, *176*
  potato, 82
  with South African culture, 142
  world, 54–55, *173*
White flour, 12
Whole-wheat breads
  basic, 92
  batter, 152
  with flax, 101
  muffins, 126
  100 percent, 141
  saluf, 138
  waffles, 165
Whole-wheat flour, 12–13
Wing, Daniel, 36, 73
Winter wheat, 12
World bread
  basic, 54–55, *173*
  durum, 97
  with soy, 108

Yeast
  commercial, xi, 2, 3
  discovery of, xii, 2
  species of, 2–3
  wild, xi, 3, 4–5
Yukon flapjacks, 157
Yukon sourdough culture, 157, 166,
  194–95
Yukon waffles, 166

About the Author

Ed Wood is a physician and research scientist. Growing up in a family imbued with a love for wildlife led to a degree in fish and game management at Oregon State University. He pursued a Ph.D. at Cornell University, where he studied under Dr. Clive McCay, one of the foremost pioneers in nutrition research in the United States, and Dr. Peter Olafson, an equal authority in animal pathology. From Cornell, Dr. Wood joined the U.S. Fish and Wildlife Service, where he was involved in basic research on the pathology of trout and salmon. The challenging field of pathology drew him to the University of Washington and a degree of doctor of medicine, followed by a residency in human pathology.

During these years, the organisms of sourdough that produced man's bread for five thousand years captured his imagination. In 1983 Dr. Wood became chairman of pathology at a new hospital for the Saudi Arabian National Guard at Riyadh. Knowing that the Middle East was the historic birthplace of bread, he began a quest for sourdough cultures passed down through generations of bakers from the beginning of civilization. His adventures, ranging from the humorous to the serious, produced a collection of sourdoughs from around the world, some dating back to antiquity.

When he returned to the United States, he brought those cultures with him, along with all of the sourdough recipes he had encountered. Four years and hundreds of baking experiments later, he produced the first edition of *World Sourdoughs from Antiquity,* the first book to combine valid science with the art of sourdough. Today, from his ranchland in the mountains of central Idaho, he continues to research new developments in sourdough baking and supplies wild sourdough cultures for avid bakers around the world. He says he is the only rancher to raise wild yeast and lactobacilli instead of livestock.